WHERE TO FISH:
Lancashire Coarse Fisheries

Martin Salisbury

Published by Sigma Leisure – an imprint of
Sigma Press, 1 South Oak Lane, Wilmslow, Cheshire SK9 6AR, England.

British Library Cataloguing in Publication Data
A CIP record for this book is available from the British Library.

ISBN: 1-85058-737-X

Typesetting and Design by: Sigma Press, Wilmslow, Cheshire.

Printed by: MFP Design & Print

Cover Design: Sid Richards

Map Design: Morag Perrott

Foreword

Today life has changed quite dramatically since I started angling in 1941. In the 1940s and 50s, angling was very accessible for the beginner or experienced angler living in London and the South East of England. Most towns and cities had several angling clubs. Most of these clubs had a charabanc or coach trip every week or perhaps a fortnight. Through the local tackle shop you could find out where the coach stops were in your town.

Come Sunday morning anglers would be gathered at these stopping points. As the coaches arrived, a loud voice would shout, "Thames at Richmond" or the "Medway at Yalding". Then it might be the "Stour at Grove Ferry" or perhaps "Leybourn Lake at West Malling". All venues were very accessible in those days. We didn't think we needed a book to show us where it was possible to fish.

In 1954, Bernard Venables gave us the *Guide to Angling Waters in South-East England*. My friends and I soon realised there were many angling venues we did not know about. We quickly searched many of them out, where we enjoyed some wonderful days at the waterside, often catching big fish.

In 1998, Martin Salisbury in a small way followed in the footsteps of Bernard Venables by writing a 36-page booklet simply titled *Coarse Fisheries in Lancashire*. For the second time in my life I realised that Lancashire had more fisheries than I was aware of. It was also an excellent guide for the beginner to angling who wanted to know where they could cast a line.

The booklet was so well received by the anglers of Lancashire that a publisher of guide books for walkers, Sigma Press, realised the value of a bigger and a more comprehensive book for anglers was needed. Martin was asked to undertake the task which has resulted in an excellent guide to Coarse Fisheries in Lancashire.

As an angler for nearly sixty years, I thoroughly recommend this book to all anglers. Not just the beginner to our wonderful sport but to anglers of sixty years experience. I am sure everyone will find something new in this latest edition of *Coarse Fisheries in Lancashire* and in turn get more enjoyment from their sport.

Martin James, presenter of BBC Radio Lancashire's 'From the Water's Edge'.

Preface

As anglers, we all have a favourite place in which to fish. Whether it is a stillwater, length of canal or a steady glide of river every angler has a place to turn to when they wish to spend a relaxing day on the bank.

However, there are many reasons why anglers will desert their favoured haunt for pastures new. Some like testing their skills on a variety of waters, others prefer a fresh challenge or perhaps their favourite venue is not what it used to be. Whatever the reason, if you are looking for a new venue to fish, this guide is an absolute must.

Not only will the content of the book help local anglers learn more about the fishing in their area, it will be an invaluable assistance to visiting anglers in locating a water to fish.

With so many fisheries to write about I have restricted myself to detailing venues within the current Lancashire boundaries. Some of you may be surprised about what is and isn't currently in Lancashire, I know it has caused some confusion while writing the guide. In producing directions to the fisheries, I used Philip's Street Atlas of Lancashire and for anyone intending to visit several of the waters I can recommend the map highly. It is available in most good bookshops.

You should remember that the book is only intended as a guide and although the prices and rules were correct at the time of enquiry they may have altered since. Although there will have been changes since I gathered my information I think you will find that most of the information is relative – i.e. expensive fisheries will still be expensive places to fish (only the price will be higher!) and those holding the bigger fish will probably still do so.

I have had to rely on fishery owners, those who run angling clubs, tackle shops and anglers themselves to compile the information in this book. I am grateful to them all but it may mean that some of the information is incorrect or misleading. Average or top fish weights may be inaccurate or the stock may not be as listed. I have tried to be as accurate as possible but as anglers yourselves you should be familiar with the: "It was this big, honest. You should have seen the size of it, it was at least 20lb!" I had to develop the art of deciphering the true comments from the exaggerated and I hope those who are not quoted as accurately as they would have liked are not offended.

Another problem area has been the ratings for disabled access. I have tried to keep the view as simplistic as possible – i.e. Poor/Average/Good/Excellent. I have also included a commentary where appropriate. In rating the disabled access I have often had to rely heavily on other people's opinions. I hope that by taking the fisheries rated Poor and eliminating them you can visit any others that interest you and assess them for yourselves.

The best source of information has come from anglers themselves. They are the ones who fish the water and know its moods and likes and dislikes better than anyone else. If you're looking for advice on fisheries in a certain area or are on a new water and are struggling, don't be afraid to ask. But remember please be polite.

It is amazing how quickly things can change. In the process of writing this book, one fishery I had gathered information on and written about was netted and sold to developers. In fact, the land has probably been built on by now. The owners of their new home will be blissfully unaware that beneath their house was once a pond that provided endless hours of enjoyment for so many. However, all is not lost as I know of other fisheries that are planned for the future or are under construction. Unfortunately, the publication date came too soon for me to provide details on them. Perhaps you can try to emulate my efforts and find them yourselves!

There are several fisheries situated in Lancashire that are not included in this guide. There are several reasons why waters have been omitted. The main one is that owners are publicity shy and prefer not to advertise their water. They feared that advertising would bring hoards of anglers and a mountain of trouble to their water. Please if you visit one of the fisheries after seeing it in this book treat it with the respect it deserves. Another reason may be that I don't know about the fishery yet. A major problem was locating the controlling body on some waters, especially the rivers. If I have been unable to locate the complete fishing rights to venues I have at least tried to provide you with a starting point.

Sadly, litter and the behaviour of anglers was a common theme of complaint amongst owners of fisheries and those involved in angling clubs. I should not need to remind anglers to act courteously, obey rules and not drop litter but please can all those who go fishing make an effort to respect the countryside and those around them. It disappoints me to hear fishery owners turn down my requests for fear of what publicity may do to their water. At the end of the day we are damaging our own image and our own sport. Like most other problems, it is a minority causing the trouble, but their actions reflect on all of us. As anglers we must do everything to protect our sport from those who criticise it.

The response to my original version of "Coarse Fisheries in Lancashire" was so overwhelming that producing an updated version became a realistic goal, and thanks to Sigma Press, the guide is now available to a wider audience. Despite the greater coverage angling in Lancashire will get through these pages I hope that a swarm of anglers will not suddenly descend on the area. If they do, you'll find me hiding in what was once a quiet corner of my favourite lake!

I hope the guide provides you with the inspiration to try new waters and leads to many more fish on the bank. In writing this book I've landed new personal best carp and pike, re-discovered the urge to fish some waters of old and found some fantastic new places I can't wait to have a crack at. I hope that you can now share some of my success and enthusiasm to get out on to the bank through these pages. Now I've finished the guide and have got more time to go fishing you might not hear of me again.

Tight lines!

Martin Salisbury.

Acknowledgements

My thanks go to all those who bought the original version of "Coarse Fisheries in Lancashire" and made it the success that it is today. To those who made the first edition possible; thank you. Grateful thanks go to all the tackle shops that stocked the first edition and assisted in production of the second. Most are listed throughout the pages of this book.

In producing this book, I would like to thank Greg Knight and Dominic George for their artwork, Martin James for his wonderful support, Michelle for her navigation of Lancashire and everyone who provided photographs. Grateful thanks to Eileen Metcalf for her proof-reading and computer skills. Thanks also to all those who answered my questions and replied to my phone calls and requests and did so in such a helpful manner.

For Mum and Dad, Lisa, Vicki and Anthony.

Publisher's Note

This book is intended to be the definitive guide to coarse fishing venues in Lancashire. Great effort has gone into compiling the information and we hope that it will be of invaluable assistance to you. However, in producing a book of this nature some information will change quickly and it is very difficult to maintain fully accurate information. By their very nature some fisheries are changing owners, rules, stocks and prices rapidly as people try to make a financial success of their dreams. Other waters have remained in the same hands for many years and will remain so for years to come.

All information included in this book was correct at the time of enquiry. We are anxious to keep the information up-to-date so if you are a fishery owner who has been omitted or know of changes that might be made to this book, do not hesitate to contact us.

Contents

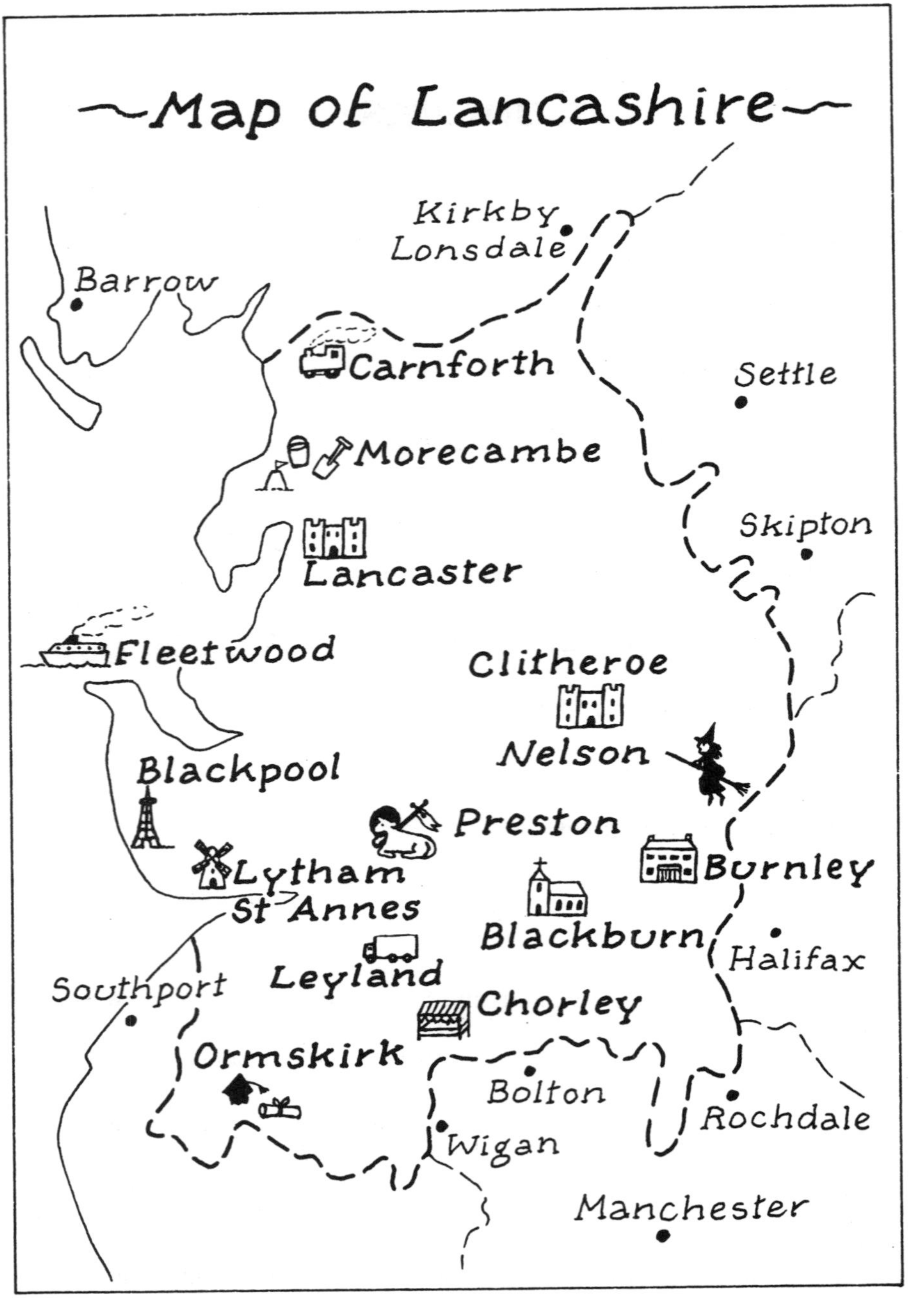

~Map of Lancashire~

Barrow

Kirkby Lonsdale

Carnforth

Settle

Morecambe

Skipton

Lancaster

Fleetwood

Clitheroe

Nelson

Blackpool

Preston

Burnley

Lytham St Annes

Blackburn

Halifax

Southport

Leyland

Chorley

Ormskirk

Bolton

Rochdale

Wigan

Manchester

Introduction

The Environment Agency

The Environment Agency is responsible for protecting and managing waterways and their surrounding countryside or area. The role they fulfil is a varied one. They deal with our water resources. The Agency control and monitor the level of water abstraction allowed in this country. They help prevent water pollution and deal with it if it occurs. They monitor the quality of water in our lakes, reservoirs and rivers. They have a major role in flood defence in this country, protecting our coastline and riverbanks from flood and erosion. The Agency also deals with the navigation of boats on our waterways.

However, the area that concerns us most as anglers is the Environment Agency's role in conservation, recreation and fisheries. The Agency plays an active role in encouraging conservation of our waterways. They provide some fishing rights for us to use. They maintain, improve and develop fisheries. They are available for advice for fishery owners and the Agency's permission is often necessary before fisheries can carry out certain developments, including re-stocking and fish movement.

The most important control the Agency has in relation to coarse anglers in this country is the requirement for an Environment Agency Rod Licence and the management of close seasons on waters.

Who needs a Rod Licence?

Anybody over the age of 12 years who fishes with a rod or line for salmon, trout or freshwater fish and eels in England or Wales is required to be in the possession of a valid Environment Agency Rod Licence.

There are two types of licence: a Salmon and Sea Trout and a Non-Migratory Trout and Coarse Fish. The Salmon and Sea Trout licence is also valid for Non-Migratory Trout and Coarse Fish but is more expensive therefore if you only intend to fish for coarse fish then you are advised to obtain the cheaper Non-Migratory Trout and Coarse Fish licence.

It does not matter whether you are fishing in a private or public water, you must be in possession of a valid rod licence. Even if the fishery were your own, you would still require a licence in order to be able to fish it legally. The Rod Licence does not permit you to fish any water. You must still seek the owner's permission before commencing fishing.

The licence allows you to fish for coarse fish with two rods at once. If you wish to fish with more you would require a second licence. By law, you are only permitted to use a maximum of four rods in pursuit of coarse fish and most fishery owners do not allow the use of so many rods anyway.

What if I go fishing without a Rod Licence?

The Environment Agency has bailiffs who visit waters, checking that anglers have the appropriate licence. You must produce your rod licence for inspection when requested to do so by an authorised person. If you are caught without a licence or are using more rods than your licence permits then you could be prosecuted and fined. The maximum fine that the courts may impose is £2,500.

The Environment Agency has increased its campaign against anglers who fish without a licence. Following publicity campaigns reminding anglers of the need for a licence the Agency have checked more anglers than ever before and prosecuted those who have failed to produce a valid licence.

Where can I purchase my Rod Licence?

You can buy a Rod Licence that lasts a full season and runs annually from April 1st, an 8-day licence, or a 1-day licence. All licences can be purchased from your local Post Office. With over 17,000 Post Offices supplying the Rod Licence you should never be caught without one.

The Environment Agency also run a telephone service that allows you to purchase a full season licence that immediately becomes valid. You pay by using your debit/credit card and then you are issued with your licence number in case you are asked to produce your licence before you have received it.

The telephone sales service is available between 8am-8pm, Monday to Sunday, which is a very convenient service to have. The number is 0870 1662662.

The current Rod Licence prices are as follows:

Full Season from 1st April to 31st March	£19.00
Full Season Concessionary	£9.50
8-Day	£6.50
1-Day	£2.50

Please Note: the prices are constantly under review and may be increased in the future.

What about the close season?

There are slight variations depending on which region you are fishing in and there are also some statutory exceptions so you should always check with the Environment Agency Regional Office, details are provided on the reverse of your Rod Licence.

In the area covered by this book, you are not permitted to fish rivers, streams or drains for coarse fish between the 15th March and 15th June inclusive. You can fish on the canals, lakes and reservoirs in the North West region. .

Please remember that some fisheries still operate the old close season (15th March-15th June inclusive) or some form of close season even though they are not required to do so by law. Other fisheries insist on a keepnet ban for the duration of the old close season. Please check before commencing fishing.

The rules regarding the close season and other bylaws are always under review and it is hoped that one day the regulations can be standardised throughout the country and that lakes, rivers and canals can share uniform rules. A full set of fisheries laws and bylaws can be obtained from your regional office.

The Environment Agency North West Regional Office

The North West Regional Office can be contacted at:

The Environment Agency, Richard Fairclough House, Knutsford Road, Warrington, WA4 1HG. Tel: 01925 653999; Fax: 01925 415961

General Enquiry Line: 0645 333111

Emergency Hotline: 0800 807060

The 24-hour emergency hotline number is for reporting all environmental incidents relating to air, land and water. Use this Freephone number if you see pollution, poaching, fish in distress, or any risks to wildlife.

To check the level of your river including the Ribble and Lune, telephone the Environment Agency North West River Level Line: 0906 6197733

Environment Agency Web Site

You can seek further information and press releases from the Agency at www.environment-agency.gov.uk

Key for Maps

⬭	Pond, Lake or River
⊢ – ⊣	Designated Fishing Areas
x x x x	No Fishing Areas
🪱	Tackle and Bait Shop
🐦	Nature Reserve
▭	Building
P	Car Park
=	Road
= = =	Track
+++++	Railway
⧓	Bridge
⚡	Electricity Pylons
🗑	Refuse Tip
⛵	Yacht Club
🛏	Bed and Breakfast
🍴	Self-Catering Accommodation
🚐	Caravan Site
Λ	Camping
♀♀	Trees

An A to Z of The Fisheries

ALAMAR RESERVOIR
Copse Road, Fleetwood.

This venue is more commonly referred to as the Fleetwood Reservoir. It is run by the Reservoir Angling Club and can be found almost in the centre of the town and only about a mile from the sea.

The reservoir is stocked with carp to 18lb, bream to 11lb, tench, rudd, roach and perch. The carp average around 7lb and the bream around 3lb. Most of the tench caught are in the 1lb-2lb bracket. There are some big eels present and there are specimens in the 3lb-5lb range regularly caught. The club hopes to introduce some chub and barbel in the near future.

The reservoir is approximately one and three quarter acres and has 40 pegs. The reservoir is between 10ft and 12ft in most places. It was originally used to fill the steam engines of the steam trains that came to the port of Fleetwood. As technology advanced, it fell into disuse and it now benefits the anglers.

Juniors are particularly welcome at the club. On many waters, an adult must accompany you, but the club insists that this is not the case on their reservoir in order to encourage the future of angling.

Cost: Season permits are £12 for adults and £11 for juniors and OAP.

Tickets: Available from Noah's Ark, 41 Lower Green, Poulton-le-Fylde. FY6 7EJ. Tel: 01253 885684. Open Mon-Sat 8am-5.30pm. Cast N Catch Angling, 7 Ash Street, Fleetwood. Tel: 01253 776151. Open Mon-Tues 9am-1pm, 2pm-5.30pm, Wed 9am-2pm, Thurs-Sat 9am-1pm, 2pm-5.30pm, Sun 9am-12pm. Bob's Tackle Shop, 35 Beach Road, Thornton-Cleveleys. Tel: 01253 860616. Open Mon-Tues 9am-5pm, Wed 9am-1pm, Thurs-Sat 9am-5pm. Mr Discount, 3 Anchorsholme Lane East, Thornton-Cleveleys. Tel: 01253 828800. Open Mon-Sat 9am-5.30pm, Sun 1am-3pm.

Rules: No bloodworm or boilies. No night fishing.

Close season: There is a two-month close season each year around April and May. The precise dates vary.

Disabled Access: Average. Wheelchair access is poor. There is one disabled peg.

Matches: The club runs matches every Friday between 7pm-9pm and every other Sunday. Junior teams fish on Saturdays. Junior teams are invited to come and fish the reservoir by prior arrangement.

Car Parking: There is a car park accommodating 200 cars alongside the reservoir.

Toilets: None.

Other Facilities: None.

Nearby Amenities: Fleetwood Freeport shopping complex is just around the corner.

Directions: Following the signs to Fleetwood Freeport take the A585 to Fleetwood. After the first roundabout you reach in Fleetwood, take the next left down Copse Road. The reservoir is on your right between the Fishermans Friend factory and the David Hallsall's toy factory.

Contact: Secretary Terry Palmer can be contacted on 01253 873209.

BAILRIGG LAKE
Scotforth, Lancaster.

This 40-peg lake is available to members of the Lonsdale Angling Club and it boasts carp to mid-double figures, tench to 7lb, roach, rudd, perch and a few bream.

The carp average between 7lb and 10lb and the tench have an average weight of 4lb. The roach are particularly plentiful.

Cost: Membership is £25 per season. Before you become a new member of the Lonsdale Angling Club you must have obtained written permission from the Membership Secretary, Lonsdale A.C., 33 Bridge Road, Greaves, Lancaster. LA1 4UL.

Tickets: Once you have been granted permission to join the club you can purchase your club card from Gerry's of Morecambe, 5-7 Parliament Street, Morecambe. Tel: 01524 422146. Open Mon-Sat 9am-5pm, Sun 9am-12pm. Morecambe Angling Centre, Grand Garage, Thornton Road, Morecambe. Tel: 01524 832332. Open every day including Bank Holidays (except Christmas Day, Boxing Day and New Years Day) Mon-Sat 9am-5.30pm, Sun 9am-12pm. Charlton and Bagnall, 3/5 Damside Street, Lancaster. Tel: 01524 63043. Open Mon-Fri 9am-5.30pm, Sat 9am-5pm, Sun 9.30am-12.30pm. Stephen Fawcett, 7 Great John Street, Lancaster. Tel: 01524 32033. Open Mon-Sat 9am-5pm. Closed Wednesdays.

Rules: A full set of rules is provided in the club card. They include no tiger nuts, peanuts or radio-controlled boats.

Close season: Open all year.

Disabled Access: Poor.

Matches: Club matches only.

Car Parking: There is parking available in the roadside lay-by.

Toilets: None.

Other Facilities: None.

Nearby Amenities: There are shops and pub about a mile away.

Directions: You are not allowed onto this venue until you are in possession of your membership card. The directions to the venue, which can be found on the outskirts of Lancaster in the Scotforth area, are found on the club card.

BALLGROVE LAKE
Winewall, near Colne.

This 25-peg lake run by the Pendle Leisure Services is an award-winning venue for its disabled facilities. It contains skimmers, roach, perch, gudgeon, tench and carp. The carp are now up to around the 20lb mark and the tench and perch have been caught at top weights of about 5lb and 3lb respectively.

Cost: Season tickets are £18.70 for adults (a second rod costs an extra £9.35) and £10 for juniors and OAP (second rod costs £5). Day tickets are £2.80 for adults and £1.50 for juniors and OAP with an additional rod costing £1.40 and 75p respectively.

Tickets: Both day and season tickets can be obtained from the bailiffs on the bank. The season ticket requires a passport-sized photograph for your card.

Rules: No keepnets between 15th March and 15th June. No boilies or livebaits. Members are allowed to night fish but they must pre-book at the Pendle Leisure Centre in Colne on 01282 661248.

Close season: Open all year.

Disabled Access: Very good.

Matches: Matches can be booked through Pendle Leisure Services on 01282 661230.

Car Parking: Yes.

Toilets: Yes, including a disabled toilet.

Other Facilities: There is a picnic area.

Nearby Amenities: Colne and Trawden. Wycoller Country Park. Foulridge (Lower) Reservoir, also run by Pendle Leisure Services, and Knotts Lane ponds are in Colne.

Directions: Leaving the M65 at its end, follow the A6068 through Colne. Turn right down the B6250 at a roundabout towards Trawden. Turn left down Winewall Road and left before the little bridge to go to the car park and lake.

Contact: For more information contact the Pendle Leisure Services on 01282 661230.

BANNISTER HOUSE FARM
Mere Brow, Southport.

This complex is currently made up of four lakes but has expanded quickly. The expansion could continue as there are plans for a kiddies' pool to be

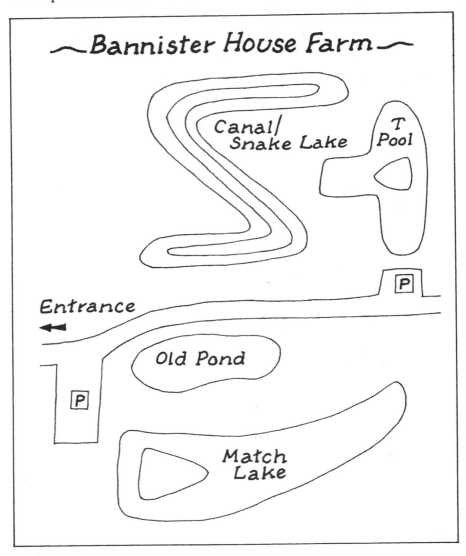

made available in the near future. It is a true mixed coarse fishery as all the most common coarse species are present except for pike and barbel.

The old pond is the first lake you see on entry to the fishery as it is directly in front of you. It is up to 6ft deep and contains carp to 9lb, tench to 5lb, bream to 6lb, crucians, roach, rudd, perch, gudgeon and hybrids. It even contains a rogue trout! There are 16 pegs on the old pond.

Next to the old pond, on your right, is the match lake. It is 4ft deep, but has a central channel which is 8ft deep with an even deeper spot that can be pinpointed by plumbing accurately in the correct area. The match lake is full of fish with carp, crucian/carp hybrids, tench, bream, chub, dace, golden orfe, roach, rudd, perch, gudgeon and hybrids. The match lake holds 38 anglers and as it name suggests is used for matches but can be used by pleasure anglers when matches are not in progress.

The T pool is down the track on the left next to the second car park. It holds 32 anglers and contains all the species found in the match pool with the exception of chub, dace and golden orfe. The carp run to 26lb and the tench to 5lb. The T pool is shallower at around 3-4ft. The T pool is also used for matches but with also the canal/snake lake and the old pond there is always room for all the anglers wishing to fish the complex.

It is expected that the canal/snake lake will hold only specimen carp and tench when it is fully opened. There are plans to put in 200 double figure carp. However, these plans may change as the 62-peg 'S' shaped lake is ideal for matches. Your best bet is to ask the owner or regulars on the stocking in the lakes at the time you go to fish.

Cost: £3 a day and £6 for a night. Juniors under 12 can fish for £2. The new canal/snake lake will probably be £5 a day and £10 a night due to it holding the specimen fish.

Tickets: Pay on bank.

Rules: The owner prefers barbless hooks to be used and no nuts are allowed- i.e. peanuts, tiger nuts etc. All cars must be left on the car parks. The owner also requests that you enjoy yourself, so lets hope your catches meet your expectations!

Close season: Open all year.

Disabled Access: The old pond can be easily accessed. The top end can be fished virtually from your car on the car park but there are only a couple of swims. The T pool can be fished but it is a bit more difficult, especially when the ground is wet.

Matches: Matches are held on the waters, currently on the T pool and the match lake. This means there is always room for the pleasure angler.

Car Parking: There are two car parks. One alongside the old pool and the other further down the fishery next to the T pool.

Toilets: None.

Other Facilities: Snacks are available including tea, coffee and soft drinks.

Nearby Amenities: Southport. The Leisure Lakes, which also provides coarse fishing, is just down the road.

Directions: To find the lakes take the A565 between Southport and Preston and after following the signs for Mere Brow Leisure Lakes continue past the entrance and go through Mere Brow village until you see the sign for Bannister Farm on your right-hand side. Once on the dirt track bear left and follow the road round. Go through the farm yard and there is a small car park in front of the first two lakes or continue left and straight down to the other lakes and another car park.

Contact: For further information contact Mr T.J. Edwards on 01704 821474 or 07801 353403.

BARRETTS FARM FISHERY
Salt Pit Lane, Mawdesley.

This small pond has 14 pegs and can be a novelty to fish as you are effectively fishing from the end of the owner's lawn! Carp to double figures, roach, bream, tench, crucian, perch and gudgeon can be found in the water.

Cost: £3 for adults and £2 for under-sixteens.

Tickets: Pay at house before commencing fishing.

Rules: Dip nets before fishing, barbless or whisker barb hooks only, loosefeeding only (no groundbait), no bloodworm, joker or boilies, no particles except sweetcorn, no keepnets except in matches and under-sixteens must be accompanied by a responsible adult. You are also not allowed dogs, radios or fires on the fishery.

Close season: Open all year.

Disabled Access: Good.

Matches: A few matches are held on the water but notices giving prior notice will be displayed.

Car Parking: Some car parking is available behind the farm's garage.

Toilets: Yes

Other Facilities: None

Nearby Amenities: The owner will point you in the right direction as regards refreshments etc. The Robin Hood pub is near by. If the pond is busy, there are plenty of other fisheries in the area including Bluestones and Heskin Old Hall. Tackle and bait can be acquired from Don's Tackle, 8 Mill Street, Coppull. Tel: 01257 794040. Open Mon-Sat 8am-6pm, Sun 8am-1pm.

Directions: In the middle of Eccleston, turn off The Green at the crossroads down Doctors Lane. Follow this road past the Robin Hood pub. Salt Pit Lane is second on your left after the pub. The fishery is halfway down this road on the left and has a sign outside.

Contact: For further information telephone Mrs Cowburn on 01257 450484.

BEACON VIEW COARSE FISHERY
Back Lane, Appley Bridge.

This is one of two fisheries in the book that fall just outside the current Lancashire boundaries. However, you will have to keep on reading to discover which is the second one.

Most fisheries seem to have an interesting point that is worth mentioning but this fishery stands out from the rest because it provides you with the opportunity to catch a sturgeon under floodlights!

Now, I know what floodlights are but when it came to the sturgeon, I had to check my guide to Freshwater Fish of Britain and Europe to discover some facts about it. The sturgeon is a bottom living fish that occurs in all European coastal waters and associated river systems.

It is rare and almost unknown in British waters. The sturgeon is long and thin and can grow to over an amazing two and a half metres long and has a bony type structure. It has a long sharp snout with a small nozzle-like mouth, which is underslung and equipped with four barbels for touch.

The sturgeon in Beacon View are up to around 4ft long (over a metre) and approximately 8lb. The unusual stocking does not stop there though. There are 28 different types of coarse fish found at the fishery. There are koi carp, golden tench and golden rudd. Among the more normal species are carp to over 20lb, tench to 7lb, bream, perch, roach, rudd, chub and barbel. The carp average just into double figures.

The lake, which is about 2 acres, is around 10ft deep and holds 47 anglers at once.

Cost: Day tickets are £5. It is £3 after 5pm. Disabled anglers can fish for £3 a day. Juniors fishing with an adult may be entitled to a discount. Please ask for details.

Tickets: Available on the bank.

Rules: No night fishing. The fishery closes at 9.30pm. Please dip nets before commencing fishing. No keepnets. Loosebait only. Barbless hooks only. No bloodworm, boilies or peanuts.

Close season: Open all year.

Disabled Access: Good. Disabled persons may drive through the car park and then between the stables in order to get access which is closer to the water.

Matches: The fishery is available to clubs wishing to book a match on the water. There is always room for pleasure anglers.

Car Parking: Yes. At the entrance to the fishery.

Toilets: Yes. By the car park.

Other Facilities: None.

Nearby Amenities: There is a garden centre just before the fishery. The nearest shops are left out of the fishery and then left again onto the housing estate. The Wheatsheaf pub can be found if you turn left at the bottom of Back Lane onto Miles Lane and the Water's Edge pub is past the Wheatsheaf down Mill Lane next to the convenience store. Both pubs serve food. The nearest fisheries are Fir Tree and Charity Farm. The local tackle shop is Dream Angling Tackle and Bait, 63 Preston Road, Standish. Tel: 01257 472707. Open Mon-Sat 9am-5.30pm.

Directions: Leave the M6 at junction 27 and head for the A5209 to Wrightington and Parbold. On leaving the motorway roundabout take an immediate left down Back Lane which is opposite the petrol station. The fishery is down here on your left immediately after the garden centre. To get to the water, walk between the stables and then up to your left.

Contact: For further information contact Graham Whaite on 01257 253899 or 0403 240114.

BIRKACRE LODGES

Birkacre Road, Chorley.

These two lodges, one small and one much larger, contain a wide range of species from tench to 8lb, bream to 5lb, crucians, perch and roach to over 2lb. There were two barbel stocked into the big lodge and they are currently around the 9lb mark. There are few pike to double figures and a small number of carp in the lodges. The big lodge contains a slightly bigger stamp of fish than the smaller lodge with the tench averaging around the 3lb to 4lb mark. The bream were stocked at 2lb and are now reaching weights around 4lb and having spawned successfully, skimmer bream are now starting to show.

The lodges are run by Wigan and District A.A. If you are going to fish Wigan club waters regularly then you are advised to buy their season ticket as it is well worth the cost. The Wigan and District A.A. own many waters with the bulk of the venues being situated around the Wigan area. The season tickets run from 1st January to 31st December each year.

Cost: The Wigan and District A.A. club card costs £16 for adults, £5 for OAP and only £2 for juniors. Day tickets are £2, £1 and 30p respectively.

Tickets: Day tickets are available on the bank from the patrolling bailiffs. The club card is available from most tackle shops in Lancashire.

Rules: There is a full set of rules in the club card but they include no tin cans containing sweetcorn, luncheon meat etc. to be taken on waters, all carp must be returned immediately, no night fishing. Adults are restricted to two rods and juniors one rod.

Close season: Closed 15th March to 15th June inclusive.

Disabled Access: The small lodge has good access but the larger lodge is rated as poor.

Matches: Club matches only.

Car Parking: Car park at entrance to fishery.

Toilets: None.

Other Facilities: None.

Nearby Amenities: Chorley town centre. Tackle and bait can be acquired from Don's Tackle, 8 Mill Street, Coppull. Tel: 01257 794040. Open Mon-Sat 8am-6pm, Sun 8am-1pm.

Directions: The reservoirs can be found on the B5251, Coppull Road, on

Dave Simpson with an 18lb 2oz pike from Birkacre Lodges

your way out of Chorley. From the centre of Chorley take the B5251 down Pall Mall and follow this road right through until you reach the traffic lights at the top of a hill with Southlands High School just off to the right. Once you have gone through the lights take the second left down Birkacre Road and the car park can be found directly in front of you in the Yarrow Valley Park as the road takes a sharp right to go up Birkacre Brow.

BLUE SLATE FISHERY
Spring Lane, Samlesbury.

The main lake at this fishery is the figure of eight which is about three-quarters of an acre in size and accommodates 18 anglers. It has varying depths from 2ft-11ft. It holds carp to 18lb plus, tench and golden orfe to 4lb and chub.

The sunken pool is about half an acre and holds a maximum of six anglers. It has an island in the middle and one side of the pool goes down to 7ft and the other 11ft. It holds carp, tench, chub and golden orfe all to about 3lb.

The breast pit holds only four anglers and is much shallower than the other waters. It is about 3ft deep and holds carp to 5lb and chub.

The quarry, as its name suggests, is much deeper and goes down to 35ft. There is room for around 20 anglers and the quarry holds carp, chub, tench, golden orfe, roach and rudd. Further stockings of the quarry are a possibility.

Cost: Day tickets are £4 for a maximum of two rods.

Tickets: Tickets are available on the bank. You must ring Craig Burns on 0958 730477 to book your day ticket.

Rules: Barbless hooks only. Groundbait on the quarry only. No boilies or nuts. No night fishing. No keepnets on the figure of eight lake. An adult must accompany children.

Close season: Open all year.

Disabled Access: There is good access to the two small ponds during summer when the fields are dry otherwise access is poor.

Matches: None.

Car Parking: Yes.

Toilets: None.

Other Facilities: None.

Nearby Amenities: There is a pub at either end of Spring Lane, the Trafalgar or the Nabs Head. There is a petrol station for snacks and a KFC about a mile away. There is a Little Chef also in the area. Red Rocks Fishery is near by.

Directions: From junction 31 of the M6 at Preston follow the A59 towards Blackburn. Just before the traffic lights where the road splits for Blackburn and Clitheroe, turn right at the Trafalgar pub down Cuerdale Lane which runs alongside the petrol station. Take the first left down Spring Lane and the fishery is one mile down here on your left.

Contact: For further information contact Craig Burns on 0958 730477 or 01254 381575 (evenings).

BLUESTONES FISHERY
Blue Stone Lane, Mawdesley.

This a very pleasant fishery that is well looked after by its owners. There is a pond and a lake that can be found at this venue. The lake is on the right-hand side and accommodates 12 anglers. It averages around 5ft deep. There are mirror and common carp to 16lb, tench to 5lb plus, bream, roach, rudd, perch, crucians and champion sized gudgeon! There are plenty of smaller fish but if you persevere with baits and tactics aimed at the better quality fish then you should not be disappointed.

The lake has an island that provides plenty of features to fish too. The lake is full of reeds and lilies which provide cover for the fish but also help divide the swims and prevent other anglers encroaching into your peg. This is particularly helpful on busy days.

The smaller pond has the same mix of fish, all of similar top weights as the lake. It has room for only five anglers and reaches depths of 14ft as it is an old well. However, it does not seem to be as heavily fished as the main lake and so, if action is slow, a few hours on the pond could provide you with greater rewards. There are overhead cables above the pond and for your safety, the owners have taken the adequate measure of allowing only float fishing with a rod and line. Ledgering is also banned on the pond due to the small number of pegs.

Cost: Day tickets are £4 with no concessions. In summer, April-October, the use of only one rod is permitted.

Tickets: Are purchased on the bank. The owner will come round and collect your money once you commence fishing. At weekends and other peak periods, it can get very busy and therefore it is necessary to ring and book your place beforehand.

Rules: Barbless hooks only (warning:- this is strictly enforced). Fishing is from dawn until dusk. There is a security light and alarm system which detects movement at night so please do not enter the fishery before daylight or you will activate the alarm. No groundbait, loosefeeding only. Landing nets must be used at all times and must be dipped before fishing. No boilies. Fish must be handled carefully and not thrown back into the water. Under-sixteens must be accompanied by an adult. All anglers must respect the owners and their neighbours and remain as quiet as possible in the mornings. If you are looking round the fishery and do not intend to fish then please do not use the car park but park on the road and contact the owner before entering or pre-arrange your visit.

Close season: Open all year.

Disabled Access: Good. The car park is alongside the water and the surrounding area is flat.

Matches: There are a small number of matches on the water every year. Warning signs will be displayed on the gate indicating that a match is in progress.

Car Parking: You can park alongside the water. To enter the fishery, go through the gate. Please note that only those fishing may open the gate and use the car park.

Toilets: Yes.

Other Facilities: There is a caravan that may be used during bad weather. Breakfasts and snacks are provided until 1pm. Tea and coffee is available and the owner will even fill your flask for you! The owner is very honest as regards the standard of fishing at the time of your intended visit or the best baits to use, so don't be afraid to ask for advice.

Nearby Amenities: The Robin Hood pub is approximately 500 yards from the fishery to your right and the Black Bull is a similar distance on your left. There are several other fisheries in the area including Barretts and Heskin Old Hall. Tackle and bait can be acquired from Don's Tackle, 8 Mill Street, Coppull. Tel: 01257 794040. Open Mon-Sat 8am-6pm, Sun 8am-1pm.

Directions: In the middle of Eccleston, turn off The Green at the crossroads down Doctors Lane. Follow this road past the Robin Hood pub. The fishery is on your left a short distance past the garage on the corner of Salt Pit Lane. There is a telegraph pole alongside the entrance to the fishery. The water is behind the bungalow.

Contact: For further information and to book pegs for weekends call Jennifer on 01704 822321 or 07957 470283.

BOURBLES LAKES

Between Preesall and Pilling.

This group of three small lakes can only be fished by the 20 members of the Bourbles Fishing Club syndicate.

The attractive lakes contain carp, tench, bream, roach, rudd and eels.

Cost: The first year costs £200 as it includes a joining fee and then the cost per year after that is £165.

Tickets: There is a waiting list in operation. To put your name forward, write to the Membership Secretary at New Rochelle, Little Tongues Lane, Preesall, Poulton-Le-Fylde, FY6 0ED.

Rules: Issued on membership to the syndicate.

Close season: Open all year.

Disabled Access: Poor.

Matches: Club matches only.

Car Parking: You can park alongside your peg.

Toilets: None.

Other Facilities: None.

Nearby Amenities: The Preesall pits.

Directions: You can find the lakes on the A588 Preesall to Pilling Road. If you are approaching the lakes from Preesall then a short distance before you enter Pilling you will find a track on your left-hand side after the Ranchhouse Restaurant. The lakes are quite a distance up this track.

BORWICK LAKE

Borwick, near Carnforth.

This attractive gravel pit is about 11 acres and holds carp to over 28lb plus. Captures of fish over 20lb are a regular occurrence. It is estimated that one in every three captures is a 20lb plus carp. There are bream into double figures, tench, perch and roach. Eels can prove to be a nuisance in the summer months. The lake does not see much general coarse fishing nor does it encourage it as the lake caters more for the carp specimen angler. Average depth is about 8ft with a maximum of 23ft.

As the lake is primarily a carp fishing venue a small syndicate of 30 anglers is in operation. Day tickets are available but are limited to only four per day to maintain the exclusivity of the fishery. Fishing is booked in 24-hour blocks and the owner opens the gates at 8am every morning to allow you in. They are then shut and locked and will not be opened until the following morning.

The lake is a private water and so you are not allowed to walk around its banks. If you are interested in fishing the lake and would like to look around please contact the owners first, giving them plenty of notice that you wish to visit.

It is not unusual to have to book months in advance in order to fish on the day you require.

Cost: £15 for 24 hours.(Three rod limit) Fishing starts at 8am each day.

Tickets: The owner will collect your money on entry. You must pre-book your ticket before fishing.

Rules: A full list of rules will be issued on your arrival but they include the need for an unhooking mat, barbless hooks only and no particles except sweetcorn. No fish/carp pellets. No shock leaders.

Close season: The water is shut from the 31st December until the middle of March each year.

Disabled Access: Excellent. There are a number of good swims available near the car park for those who cannot walk far and the owner will help those unable to carry their own gear. Severely disabled anglers may be allowed to drive round to their peg.

Matches: None.

Car Parking: As the owners live on the water the car park is securely locked both day and night.

Toilets: Yes.

Other Facilities: None

Nearby Amenities: There is a village shop at Over Kellet. Carnforth centre is not far. Tackle and bait can be obtained from Gerry's of Morecambe, 5-7 Parliament Street, Morecambe. Tel: 01524 422146. Open Mon-Sat 9am-5pm, Sun 9am-12pm. Morecambe Angling Centre, Grand Garage, Thornton Road, Morecambe. Tel: 01524 832332. Open every day including Bank Holidays (except Christmas Day, Boxing Day and New Years Day) Mon-Sat 9am-5.30pm, Sun 9am-12pm.

Directions: The lake can be found a few minutes away from junction 35 of the M6 at Carnforth. If you follow the signposts for Over Kellet, on reaching the village green, take a left and then the next left immediately after leaving the village. The lake is down this road and can be found on the right-hand side a short distance after crossing the Lancaster Canal.

Contact: To book contact Terry or Marie Coates on 01524 720844. The telephone number should only be used as a reference for those who have fished before and wish to re-book or *serious anglers* who would like to fish the venue and are prepared to abide by the rules and respect the fishery.

BRIARCROFT FISHERY

Rawcliffe Road, St Michael's On Wyre.

A total of 30 pegs are available on this pleasant venue which can be found in the village of St Michael's on Wyre.

The two small lakes, which have depths up to about 8ft, are well stocked with carp, tench, bream, roach, rudd, perch, gudgeon and crucians. The bream and tench weigh up to around the 5lb mark, although the average weight is lower. The current best carp is just over 21lb. There are 3 known twenties in the lakes.

Cost: Fishing is by day ticket and costs £4.50 for one rod, £5.50 for two and £6.00 for three. Night fishing is permitted and costs £7.00 per night.

Tickets: Either purchase from the house or wait until the owner comes round to collect your money.

Rules: No groundbait, bloodworm or any type of nuts. Barbless hooks must be used. Keepnets are banned except in matches and all nets must be dipped before use.

Close season: Open all year.

Disabled Access: Average, although the owner will help disabled anglers to their peg which improves accessibility.

Matches: The owner holds an open match every Tuesday during summer, contact him for further details. Club matches are often held on the water on Sundays.

Car Parking: Yes.

Toilets: Yes. There are both ladies' and gents' toilets.

Other Facilities: The owner sells a small selection of fishing tackle and bait including maggots, hemp, boilies, sweetcorn, luncheon meat, hooks and floats. Also available are a wide range of snacks including bacon butties, pies, crisps, drinks and ice cream. There is a caravan site at the fishery which is a Caravan Club certified location.

A beautiful Briarcroft Common Carp for Nicholas Carter

Nearby Amenities: If the fishery is busy then try Hudsons Farm, Wyreside Fisheries or Toad Hall just down the road.

Directions: To find the fishery turn off the A6 in Bilsborrow following the signs for Myerscough College and Guy's Thatched Hamlet. Continue along this road until it ends and then turn right at the mini-roundabout before turning left onto Rawcliffe Road in the centre of the village. The fishery is situated on the left just down this road.

Contact: For further details contact Paul and Doreen Ashcroft on 01995 679289.

BUTTS MILL

Belmont Road, Great Harwood.

This is the first of seven stillwaters run by the Hyndburn and Blackburn Anglers Association who also have rights to canal fishing under the BWW scheme and three stretches of river on the Calder. The angling club has a superb selection on offer and if you join them there is plenty of fishing to keep you going all year round.

Butts Mill is a small water with room for 10 anglers. It is a steady 8ft deep and is the club's 'action' water. This is because it is stuffed full with small carp. There are also some good tench, skimmers and roach.

Cost: The Hyndburn and Blackburn Angling Association club card costs £38 for seniors, £21 for disabled and £13 for juniors and OAP.

Tickets: The club card is available from Leonard's Angling, 5 Whalley Road, Clayton-le-Moors, Accrington. Tel: 01254 231148. Open Mon-Sat 9am-5pm, Sun 8.30am-11.30am. Roe Lee Tackle Box, 336 Whalley New Road, Blackburn. Tel: 01254 676977. Open Mon-Sat 9am-5.30pm. Angler's Den, 19 Blackburn Road, Darwen. Tel: 01254 706713. Open Mon-Sat 9.30am-5pm. Hyndburn Angling Centre, 71 Abbey Street, Accrington. Tel: 01254 397612. Open Mon-Tues 9am-5pm, Wed 9am-12pm, Thurs 9am-5pm, Fri-Sat 9am-5.15pm. Geoff Done's Fishing Tackle Shop, 12 Southworth Street, Blackburn. Tel: 01254 698161. Open Mon-Thurs 9am-5.30pm, Fri 9am-6pm, Sat 9am-5pm.

Rules: One rod only.

Close season: Open all year.

Disabled Access: Good.

Matches: Club matches only.

Car Parking: Roadside car parking.

Toilets: None.

Other Facilities: None.

Nearby Amenities: The water is almost in the centre of Great Harwood. The nearest tackle shop is Leonard's see address above.

Directions: If you take the B6535 through Great Harwood then turn down Delph Road and then onto Belmont Road the water is on your left.

RIVER CALDER

Despite being a tributary of the mighty Ribble, the River Calder is a fantastic fishery in its own right. The quality and diversity of its fishing is noteworthy and it has been providing some very consistent sport for its anglers.

There are plenty of chub in the river with most of the fish caught being up to the 4lb mark. There are plenty of fish around the 2lb mark and these 'chublets' as they have been nicknamed provide some super sport all year round. The stock of chub is supplemented by barbel, dace, roach, gudgeon, perch, pike and the beautiful grayling. The river provides some good dace fishing with specimens up to a pound a distinct possibility.

The Hyndburn and Blackburn A.A. provide some of the best access to the river, controlling three stretches of the Calder. The first is at Simonstone and it provides good all round coarse fishing. If you are after pike then this is the best of their three stretches in which to pursue the toothy predator.

The second stretch is at Dunkirk Farm at Read and the third stretch is at Whalley on both banks by the Abbey near Billington caravans. The Whalley stretch is particularly noted for its grayling. There are not many places in Lancashire where you can fish for grayling so it might be worth obtaining the Hyndburn and Blackburn club card if you fancy catching one of our less common coarse species.

The Pendle and District A.A. have a stretch spanning three-quarters of a mile at Padiham. This has been producing some good sport.

The Accrington and District Fishing Club has a length between the Martholme Viaduct downstream to the Cock Bridge opposite the garden centre. This area is worth visiting if you are after the chub.

The Prince Albert AS control a stretch of the Calder by Holehouse Farm at Whalley.

Cost: The Hyndburn and Blackburn Angling Association club card costs £38 for seniors, £21 for disabled and £13 for juniors and OAP.

Season tickets for the Pendle and District A.A. are £12 for one rod with an extra rod costing an additional £8.

Membership to the Accrington and District Fishing Club coarse section is £40 for seniors and £6 for juniors.

Membership to the Prince Albert AS is £66.

Tickets: The Hyndburn and Blackburn A.A. club card is available from most East Lancashire tackle shops, see Butts Mill for details.

Pendle and District A.A. cards are available from Mack's Tackle, 33a Parliament Street, Burnley. BB11 3JU. Tel: 01282 427386. Open Mon-Wed 9am-5.30pm, Thurs 9.30am-6pm, Fri 9am-6pm, Sat 9am-5pm. Hyndburn Angling Centre, 71 Abbey Street, Accrington. Tel: 01254 397612. Open Mon-Tues 9am-5pm, Wed 9am-12pm, Thurs 9am-5pm, Fri-Sat 9am-5.15pm.

Accrington and District Fishing Club membership is available from Leonard's Angling, 5 Whalley Road, Clayton-le-Moors, Accrington. Tel: 01254 231148. Open Mon-Sat 9am-5pm, Sun 8.30am-11.30am. Roe Lee Tackle Box, 336 Whalley New Road, Blackburn. Tel: 01254 676977. Open Mon-Sat 9am-5.30pm. Hyndburn Angling Centre see address above.

There is a three-year waiting list for membership to the Prince Albert AS. If you want to join the list, write to the Membership Secretary at 37 Sherwood Road, Macclesfield, Cheshire. SK11 7RR. Please include a stamped addressed envelope so that the Membership Secretary can confirm by return of post that you have been added to the list.

Close season: The river is closed 15th March to 15th June inclusive.

CHARITY FARM
Eccleston.

This venue seems very popular as there are always plenty of people fishing when I visit the water. There are three ponds and a fourth water is under construction and should be ready for the year 2000 season. Fishing is allowed from dawn until dusk.

The first pond has 20 pegs and has an average depth of 5ft although it goes down to 10ft deep. It holds carp to 20lb, tench to 4lb, roach, rudd and perch to 1lb, chub to 2lb and bream to 5lb. The water holds plenty of skimmer bream.

The second pond has 10 pegs and is around 4ft deep. The pond is especially good for tench to 4lb. It also contains carp to 10lb, roach and perch to over 1lb and rudd.

Pond 3 is smaller and it is possible to fit in 10 anglers at a squeeze. Despite its size, it holds carp to 15lb, bream to 5lb, perch to 2lb, roach and rudd to 1lb and gudgeon.

The fourth water will be bigger than any of the current ponds and hold over 30 pegs. It will have the same mix of fish that are found in the other ponds. The addition of the new lake will certainly ease the pressure on the other ponds and make this venue an even more attractive place to fish.

Cost: £4 per person per day. Extra rods are £1 each. An adult and child under 10 sharing the same peg using one rod each costs £5 and an adult and child under 10 using one rod each but separate pegs is £6. There will be an additional charge of £1 if you have not complied with the self-pay system.

Tickets: A self-pay system is in operation and the pay cabin is situated alongside pond 1.

Rules: No night fishing, keepnets, litter or excessive noise. Groundbait in

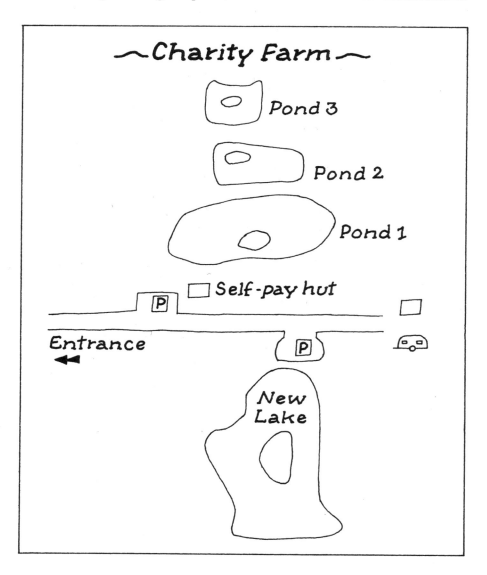

moderation and barbless hooks only. Young children should be accompanied by an adult and kept under control. Dogs should be kept on a short lead.

Close season: Open all year.

Disabled Access: Good. With prior arrangement with the owner, good access to the lakes can be arranged. Access may well be better on the new lake.

Matches: Matches are held throughout the year but only one lake is used at once so there is always room for pleasure anglers.

Car Parking: The car park for the fishery is signposted on the left as you go up the track.

Toilets: Yes.

Other Facilities: There is a vending machine selling tea and coffee, crisps, chocolate and soft drinks. There is room for touring caravans on site and these get very busy at weekends so it is essential to book in advance at weekends and peak periods.

Nearby Amenities: The Brook House pub is opposite the entrance to Charity Farm. Eccleston with its shops and pubs is not far either. There are also Camelot, Bygone Times, Cedar Farm and Eccles Farm tourist attractions in the area. Tackle and bait can be acquired from Don's Tackle, 8 Mill Street, Coppull. Tel: 01257 794040. Open Mon-Sat 8am-6pm, Sun 8am-1pm.

Directions: To find the fishery follow the signposts for Camelot and Bygone Times and leave the A49, Preston Road, as instructed. Pass Camelot and when you reach the end of Park Hall Road turn right towards the centre of Eccleston. Soon after passing Bygone Times on the left and Pontins headquarters on the right you need to turn left down Bannister Lane. Follow this road and eventually you will reach the Brook House pub on your left. The fishery is a short distance past the pub on the right.

Contact: For further information contact Fred Waring on 01257 451326.

CLARENDON STREET RESERVOIR
Plantation Street, Accrington.

This reservoir is quite unusual in that it starts at just over a foot deep at one end and slopes off to finish around 14ft deep at the other.

The reservoir is run by Hyndburn and Blackburn A.A. and it has 16 pegs. It holds good stocks of carp, roach, perch, gudgeon and chub.

Cost: The Hyndburn and Blackburn Angling Association club card costs £38 for seniors, £21 for disabled and £13 for juniors and OAP.

Tickets: The club card is available from most East Lancashire tackle shops, see Butts Mill for details.

Rules: One rod only.

Close season: Open all year.

Disabled Access: Good.

Matches: None.

Car Parking: Roadside parking only.

Toilets: None.

Other Facilities: None.

Nearby Amenities: The reservoir is close to the centre of Accrington. As well as the Slates Pits, which can be found at the end of Plantation Street, other Hyndburn and Blackburn A.A. waters in the area include Fern Gore and Kerns Allen. Hyndburn Angling Centre, 71 Abbey Street, Accrington. Tel: 01254 397612. Open Mon-Tues 9am-5pm, Wed 9am-12pm, Thurs 9am-5pm, Fri-Sat 9am-5.15pm.

Directions: The reservoir can be found off the A680, Eastgate, down Plantation Street in Accrington. At the set of traffic lights on Eastgate, turn left onto Plantation Street. A right turn at the same set of traffic lights will take you onto Abbey Street where you can find the Hyndburn Angling Centre who will be able to help if you cannot find the reservoir.

CLAYLANDS CARAVAN SITE
Off A6, between Cabus and Forton.

Fishing on the caravan site's four ponds is allowed between 8.30am and dusk all year round. The ponds, which can accommodate about 10 anglers each, hold carp, tench, bream, roach, crucians and perch. The ponds are predominantly stocked with carp which average 1lb to 3lb but there are specimens just into double figures present. The ponds are very deep in some places with depths ranging from 3-15ft.

Cost: Day tickets cost £4.50 for adults and £2 for under-sixteens. If you want to use a second rod, it costs an extra £1.

Tickets: You must pay at the shop before commencing fishing.

Rules: You are not allowed to use keepnets, bread based groundbait, boilies or barbed hooks.

Close season: Open all year.

Disabled Access: Good. Wheelchair access is available to two of the ponds.

Matches: None.

Car Parking: You may drive to your peg to drop off your gear but then you are required to park outside the shop at the entrance.

Toilets: Yes. There is also a disabled toilet.

Other Facilities: The caravan site has pitches available for both static and touring caravans and there are good on site facilities which include a well-stocked shop.

Nearby Amenities: There are several other fisheries in the area including Cleveley Bridge, Wyreside and Thursland Hill Farm.

Directions: The ponds can be found directly off the A6 between Cabus and Forton. The caravan site is well signposted on the A6, with a picture of a caravan and tent with the wording Claylands which clearly identifies the caravan site. Once you have turned off the A6 follow the track over the hill and you will then drop into the caravan site.

Contact: For more information contact Fred or Alan Robinson on 01524 791242.

CLEVELEY BRIDGE FISHERY

Near Scorton.

The 15 lakes found on this complex hold a wide variety of fish including barbel, which you would normally associate with running water. There are only a small number of barbel present but their weights range from 5lb to around 9lb so if you do connect with one you are guaranteed a large specimen. The lakes also hold carp to 28lb, tench to 8lb, bream to 12lb and chub to just over 5lb. There are also roach, rudd, perch, gudgeon, crucians and grass carp. The original lakes were dug in 1951 and, although they were not open for fishing until much later, the fishery is well established and provides pleasant surroundings in which to fish. The average depths of the lakes are between 4-6ft. The area is also a nature reserve and it is not unusual to spot Roe Deer or Kingfishers.

Cost: Fishing is £6 per day for one rod and £10 for two.

Tickets: To pay you need to go to the porch of the house and fill in the details on the front of an envelope which includes your name and car registration number. You then put your money in the envelope and post it through the door. This must be done before you commence fishing.

Rules: Barbless hooks only, no keepnets, no boilies or nut based baits and you must use a minimum line strength of 4lb (or 8lb if you are specifically fishing for carp.) Loosefeeding rather than groundbaiting is encouraged.

Close season: Open all year.

Disabled Access: Good.

Matches: None.

Car Parking: Yes, alongside the largest of the lakes.

Toilets: Yes.

Other Facilities: None.

Nearby Amenities: There is Wyreside, Woodfold Farm Fisheries,

Thursland Hill Farm, Manor House Fisheries, Copthorne, Claylands and several other fisheries off the A6.

Directions: To find the complex leave the M6 at junction 32, Broughton, and take the A6 towards Garstang. After reaching the traffic lights at Garstang exactly three-quarters of a mile further up the A6 is a sign post for Scorton and the Trough of Bowland, take this road and follow the signs for the Scorton picnic area. The fishery is a short distance on your right-hand side after you have passed the picnic area and the River Wyre. Or, alternatively, coming south from Lancaster turn off the A6 at the New Hollies pub and then take your first right.

CLIVIGER FISHPONDS

A646 at Cliviger.

These two ponds are stocked with a huge array of different species. The top pond has 28 pegs and has carp to 12lb, tench to 6lb, bream to 4lb, barbel, chub, roach, rudd, dace, gudgeon, perch and crucians. There are also the more exotic ghost and koi carp, golden tench, golden orfe and ide.

The bottom pond has roughly the same mix of fish except for the bream. The bottom pond is more noted for its carp with specimens to 20lb plus.

Both ponds have an average depth of 5ft with shallower areas present.

Cost: Day tickets are £3 for adults and £1.50 concessions. Concessions are those under 16, women, OAP (over 65), wheelchair or limbless disabled. Membership to Todmorden Angling Society allows you to fish Cliviger and several other waters just outside the Lancashire boundary. It costs £22 plus an entrance fee of £10 for adults and £11 for concessions with no entrance fee required.

Tickets: Day tickets must be purchased in advance and they are available from local tackle shops including Mack's Tackle, 33a Parliament Street, Burnley. BB11 3JU. Tel: 01282 427386. Open Mon-Wed 9am-5.30pm, Thurs 9.30am-6pm, Fri 9am-6pm, Sat 9am-5pm. They are also available from the Monarch petrol station at Cliviger. Membership to Todmorden Angling Society can be obtained at local tackle shops including Mack's Tackle or you can write to Mr R. Barber, 12 Grisedale Drive, Burnley.

Rules: Maximum of two rods. Rods must not be left unattended. Groundbait in moderation. Barbless or microbarbed hooks. No groundbaiting with boilies. No carp to be kept in keepnets. No night fishing.

Close season: Open all year.

Disabled Access: Poor.

Matches: There are a couple of club matches held on the water each season.

Car Parking: No. There is a roadside lay-by.

Toilets: No.

Other Facilities: None.

Nearby Amenities: The Monarch petrol station which sells day tickets has chocolate, crisps and snacks. Mack's Tackle – see address above. Rowley Lake, Michelin Lodge, Love Clough and Penny Lodge are nearby.

Directions: Found on the A646 Burnley to Todmorden Road at Cliviger. Taking the A646 from Burnley, after passing the Ram Inn pub there is a lay-by on your left.

CLOWBRIDGE RESERVOIR

On A682 at Clow Bridge, between Burnley and Rawtenstall.

This reservoir provides some excellent sport for the predatory pike. The current best stands at just a shade over the magical 30lb mark. Fish averaging between 15lb and 22lb are regularly caught. There are also plenty of perch present to 1lb plus and a few trout.

The reservoir is also used for sailing etc. If there are beginners' lessons being held on the water then anglers will be advised when purchasing their ticket which bank to fish. This means you can avoid having learners who don't know how to control their boat/windsurf drifting into your swim. There is plenty of bank space and so you should not have difficulty finding a peg.

Cost: Fishing costs £3.50 a day.

Tickets: Tickets can be bought from the sailing club building on the reservoir. If you are there especially early, when the shop is not open, then the bailiff will come round later and collect your money.

Close season: Open all year.

Disabled Access: Average. The disabled can access some pegs but Clowbridge is a rocky reservoir and so this makes things difficult.

Matches: None.

Car Parking: Large car park by the clubhouse.

Toilets: Yes. Situated in the clubhouse.

Other Facilities: The shop sells snacks and refreshments.

Nearby Amenities: Burnley is only a few miles away. Mack's Tackle, 33a Parliament Street, Burnley. BB11 3JU. Tel: 01282 427386. Open Mon-Wed 9am-5.30pm, Thurs 9.30am-6pm, Fri 9am-6pm, Sat 9am-5pm. Love Clough and Penny Lodge are about a mile away.

Directions: The reservoir can be found half way between Burnley and Rawtenstall on the A682.

Contact: Further information can be obtained from the Rossendale Valley Water Park shop on 01282 412965.

COPTHORNE LAKES

Nateby, near Garstang.

This venue has now been separated into two fisheries, Copthorne and Little Copthorne, although in practice the two venues can still be found side by side.

Little Copthorne is for match fishing only and comprises of two lakes. The main lake has 60 pegs and is the match carp lake. It is a mixed coarse lake that holds predominantly carp. The other 18-peg match lake is stocked with an abundance of silver fish.

Copthorne is the place that the pleasure angler should head for. The canal lake has 34 pegs. The main lake 30 pegs. The small tench pool and the ide pool both have six pegs and the bream pool has 10 pegs. Most coarse fish can be found on the venue. The carp are generally from 12oz to 5lb but there are fish up to 20lb in weight present. And there are roach, rudd, perch, chub, bream, tench, crucian carp, ide and golden orfe. If you are after a particular species, or even if you just want general advice on which lake is fishing best, don't be afraid to ask at the on site tackle shop.

Cost: Day tickets are £5 and an evening ticket available after 4pm is £3. Season tickets are available at the price of £15 per month which can be paid by standing order.

Tickets: Available from the tackle shop after 8am. If you are there earlier, you can pay on the bank when the bailiff comes round.

Rules: One rod only. No night fishing. Barbless hooks. Carp pellets/groundbait must be purchased from the on site shop.

Close season: Open all year.

Disabled Access: Excellent.

Matches: The water can be booked for matches.

Car Parking: There is ample parking alongside each water.

Toilets: Yes.

Other Facilities: Caravan hook up points and a bait shop.

Nearby Amenities: Manor House Fisheries can be found only a short distance away. Plenty of pubs and shops on the nearby A6, including The Flag pub and the Lunch Box sandwich bar.

Directions: To find the fishery take the A6 out of Preston and head towards Garstang when you reach The Flag public house turn left and go through the village of Nateby. After passing through the village, the water can be found on the right-hand side a short distance down the road.

Contact: For further information contact Derek Hallworth on 01995 601100(evenings).

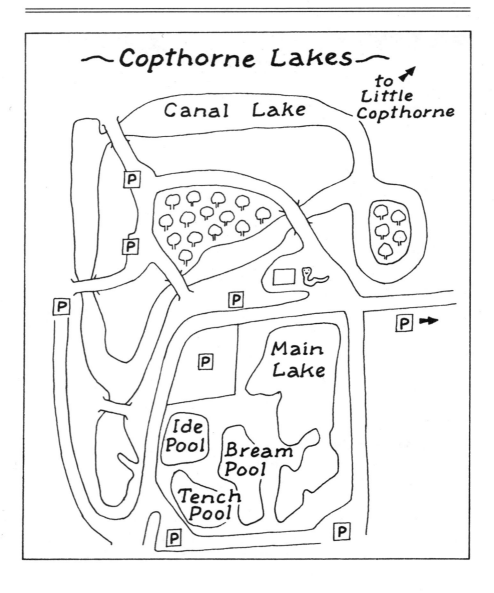

CRICKET FIELD LODGE
Off A674 at Withnell Fold.

This is the first of eight Withnell Anglers' club waters featured in this book. The club provides a mixture of club only and club/day ticket stillwaters which are well run and well bailiffed.

The Cricket Field Lodge has 30 pegs and is stocked with bream, crucians, tench, roach and perch. Junior Lodge, another Withnell Anglers' water, can be found near by.

Cost: Season tickets for Withnell Anglers are £35 for those who live within the parish of Withnell, which includes Abbey Village, Brinscall and Withnell Fold. Those who live outside the parish boundary can join as associate members for £45.

Tickets: To join the club you must apply to the Membership Secretary at PO Box 41, Chorley, PR6 8JZ. For further information contact Membership Secretary Bernard Wren on 01254 830935.

Rules: Club members only, no day tickets. Maximum of two rods. No keepnets in the close season. ALL anglers are responsible for ANY litter found within 10ft of their fishing position.

Close season: Open all year.

Disabled Access: Poor.

Matches: Club matches only.

Car Parking: None. There is room for six cars to your right when you reach the top of the lane. Please do not park on the cricket field car park.

Toilets: None.

Other Facilities: None.

Nearby Amenities: Junior Lodge and Withnell Fisheries are very close. Rakes Brook, Roddlesworth, Shale Hole and Croft Lodge are near by Withnell Anglers' waters.

Directions: Leave the M65 at junction 3 and at the roundabout take the A674 towards Higher Wheelton. You will soon reach the small village of Withnell Fold. Turn right into the village and follow the track round up to your left towards the cricket field.

CROFT FISHERIES
Adlington.

This fishery consists of three lakes which take up approximately one acre each. There are 24 pegs on the Croft Lake, 25 pegs on Huyton No. 1 and 22 pegs on Huyton No. 2.

The Croft Lake is packed with bream to 5lb, tench to nearly 4lb, crucians, roach, skimmers and the odd carp.

Huyton No. 1 Lake is mainly carp with plenty of ghost carp to around 2lb and a few larger carp with commons and mirrors to 16lb. There have been substantial stockings of bream and tench into No. 1 and these fish are starting to show well in catches. The lake is frequently stocked with small carp so sport is usually good. There are also specially constructed disabled pegs on Huyton No. 1.

Bream, tench and roach make up the stock for Huyton No. 2. The average depths of the lakes are between 3 and 4ft although Huyton No. 1 is perhaps slightly deeper with depths up to 8ft at the dam wall end.

Cost: Day tickets cost £3 for one rod for adults and £2 for juniors, disabled and OAP. There is a concessionary ticket of £2 available after 4pm. A 10-visit ticket costing £20 is available for those who visit the fishery often.

Tickets: There is a self-pay system in operation. You must use the pay office before commencing fishing.

Rules: There is no night fishing allowed and barbless hooks must be used. Other rules are no bloodworm, joker, any pellets or paste and boilies. Keepnets are banned between 31st March-15th June inclusive and nets must be dipped before use.

Close season: Open all year.

Disabled Access: Good. There are about a dozen pegs on No 1 and some pegs on No 2.

Matches: Match bookings can be made and cost £3 per peg with a £1 deposit. Only one lake will be used at once for matches leaving the other two still open for pleasure anglers.

Car Parking: Yes.

Toilets: There are toilets on site including a disabled toilet.

Other Facilities: None.

Nearby Amenities: The superb White Bear pub is 200 yards back towards Adlington. There are plenty of shops in Adlington itself. Nearest tackle shop is Crown Tackle and Bait, 4a Chorley New Road, Horwich. Tel: 01204 668223. Open Mon-Fri 9am-6pm, Wed 9am-12.30pm, Sat 9am-5.30pm.

Directions: To find the fishery taking the A6 south from Preston/Chorley. On reaching Adlington turn left alongside the Pin Croft works soon after you have passed a petrol station. Follow this newly tarmacked track and you will see the first lake on your right-hand side. There is also a cricket field down this track.

Contact: For further information contact John King on 01257 483147 or 0410 659024, or Tom on 01257 480320.

CROFT LODGE

Lodge Bank, Brinscall.

This lodge is run by the Withnell Anglers and is often referred to as Brinscall Lodge. It has 28 pegs and is relatively shallow compared to many other waters. It contains plenty of carp in the 7lb-10lb bracket. There are also bream to over 2lb, roach and perch.

The lodge supports a large head of wildfowl which can prove a nuisance at times, especially if you are trying to fish the end nearest the car park.

Cost: Season tickets for Withnell Anglers are £35 for those who live within the parish of Withnell, which includes Abbey Village, Brinscall and Withnell Fold. Those who live outside the parish boundary can join as associate members for £45.

Tickets: To join the club you must apply to the Membership Secretary at PO Box 41, Chorley, PR6 8JZ. For further information contact Membership Secretary Bernard Wren on 01254 830935.

Rules: Club members only, no day tickets. Maximum of two rods. No night fishing. ALL anglers are responsible for ANY litter found within 10ft of their fishing position.

Close season: The lodge is closed from 15th March until 15th June inclusive.

Disabled Access: Good. A few pegs can be reached directly from the car park.

Matches: Club matches only.

Potential wildfowl problems at Croft Lodge

Car Parking: There is a small car park which faces the water. Turn immediately left behind the swimming baths once on Lodge Bank.

Toilets: None.

Other Facilities: None.

Nearby Amenities: Shale Hole pond is just around the corner. The Cricket Field Lodge, Junior Lodge, Rakes Brook and Roddlesworth are other nearby Withnell Anglers' waters. You are situated almost in the centre of Brinscall so the local shops and pubs are not far away.

Directions: To find Croft Lodge leave junction 8 of the M61 and take the A674 towards Blackburn and then turn right up Briers Brow which is in front of the Dressers Arms pub. Follow this road until you reach the end and then turn right at the junction onto School Lane. This road takes you into the centre of Brinscall and you should turn right onto Lodge Bank when you have almost reached the bottom of the hill.

RIVER CROSSENS
Off A565, Southport New Road.

This river is also widely known as The Sluice and is under the control of Southport & District Angling Association. A section of The Sluice can be fished on day ticket with the rest of the river designated for members only. The club also controls the fishing on the Back Drain, which runs parallel to The Sluice, and the Three Pools. The Back Drain and Three Pools are for members only. As you can tell by the names, 'Sluice' and 'Drain', the rivers are more like canals or drains in appearance.

The Sluice, Back Drain and Three Pools provide good fishing for bream, tench, roach, perch, pike and the odd carp. There are some good pike and the Back Drain is particularly noted for this species.

Members of the club are also entitled to fish Mere Brow Leisure Lakes which is further down the A565 towards Preston and also a stretch of the River Ribble.

Cost: Day tickets for adults are £3 and juniors, OAP and disabled are £1. Membership to the club is £34 for adults, £17 for OAP and disabled and £10 for juniors.

Tickets: Day tickets can be purchased from Ted Carter's, 85-88 Church Street, Preston. Tel: 01772 253476. Open Mon-Sat 9am-5.30pm, closed Thursdays.

Membership to Southport & District Angling Association can be obtained by sending your name, address, current rod licence number and remittance to the Treasurer at 50 Lexton Drive, Southport.

Rules: The day ticket stretch runs from the Old Railway Bridge to approximately 200 yards from the pumping station at the sea end.

Close season: The river is closed 15th March to 15th June inclusive.

Car Parking: There is a car park alongside the A565 on your right-hand side.

Directions: The best way to locate the River Crossens is by taking the A565 to Southport and after the roundabout for Banks you cross the two rivers before reaching the main Southport roundabout. You need to turn right onto the parking before crossing the river. There are other access points to the rivers but this is the main point for the day ticket stretch.

CUERDEN VALLEY LAKE
Cuerden Valley Park, Clayton-le-Woods.

The lake contains a good mix of coarse fish including roach, gudgeon, bream, perch and small pike around the 5lb mark. A pike weighing just over 20lb was caught from this venue some years ago but the catch was so unusual that it even made headlines in the local evening newspaper. There are also some big carp in the water with reports of fish into upper double figures being made.

Cost: Day tickets are £3 for adults and £1.50 for juniors, OAP and unemployed. A half-priced ticket is available after 4.30pm. Night fishing costs £4.

Tickets: Must be purchased from Lostock Tackle Box, 16 Watkin Lane, Lostock Hall, Preston. Tel: 01772 626585. Open Mon-Thurs 7.30am-6pm, Fri 7am-8pm, Sat 6am-6pm, Sun and Bank Holidays 7am-12pm.

Close season: 15th March-15th June inclusive.

Disabled Access: Vehicle access for the disabled can be arranged. A key to the gates is available on application to the Cuerden Hall office.

Matches: Occasional matches are held on the water.

Car Parking: Two car parks situated at different ends of the park. A long walk from either car park is required.

Toilets: None.

Other Facilities: The lake is situated in the grounds of Cuerden Valley Park and so picnic benches and marked paths are provided to allow you to make use of the park.

Nearby Amenities: Lostock Tackle Box see address above. Stones Fishing Tackle Shop, 13 Golden Hill Lane, Leyland. Tel: 01772 421953. Open Mon-Tues, Thurs-Fri 9am-5.30pm, Wed 9am-12.30pm, Sat 9am-5pm.

Directions: The first car park is just out of Bamber Bridge on the A49, Wigan Road, next to the new motorway bridge. It is probably closer to the water but involves steeper gradients. To find it, leave the M6 motorway at junction 29 and head towards Bamber Bridge. At the first set of traffic lights turn left and then you will find the car park a short distance up this road on the left. The other is in Clayton-le-Woods at the bottom of Sheep Hill.

DICKENS STREET
Dickens Street, Blackburn.

Controlled by the Hyndburn and Blackburn A.A. this water holds plenty of carp and crucian carp, roach, bream, tench and perch. There have been recent re-stockings which have helped boost the existing head of fish.

There are 22 pegs on the water which is an average of just over 4ft deep.

Cost: The Hyndburn and Blackburn Angling Association club card costs £38 for seniors, £21 for disabled and £13 for juniors and OAP.

Tickets: The club card is available from most East Lancashire tackle shops, see Butts Mill for details.

Rules: One rod only.

Close season: Open all year.

Disabled Access: Average. There are four pegs that disabled anglers may be able to reach.

Matches: Club matches only.

Car Parking: Roadside parking only.

Toilets: None.

Other Facilities: None.

Nearby Amenities: The water is very close to the centre of Blackburn. The nearest tackle shop is Geoff Done's Fishing Tackle Shop, 12 Southworth Street, Blackburn. Tel: 01254 698161. Open Mon-Thurs 9am-5.30pm, Fri 9am-6pm, Sat 9am-5pm.

Directions: It can be found very close to the Leeds-Liverpool Canal at Higher Audley off the A679, Audley Range. Turn down Bennington Street which is next to the canal bridge and then onto Dickens Street.

FARINGTON LODGES
Lodge Lane, Leyland.

The lodges are actually two connected lakes which can be fished from one bank only. The bank you cannot fish from is heavily tree-lined with branches leaning over into the water and even the bank from which you fish has plenty of tree cover.

The water holds some large bream and tench. The carp are mainly in double figures although a 20lb plus fish has been caught. There are also roach, perch, crucians and some pike.

Cost: Day tickets are £2.50 for adults and £2 for juniors and OAP.

Tickets: Must be purchased from Lostock Tackle Box, 16 Watkin Lane, Lostock Hall, Preston. Tel: 01772 626585. Open Mon-Thurs 7.30am-6pm, Fri 7am-8pm, Sat 6am-6pm, Sun and Bank Holidays 7am-12pm.

Rules: Juniors must be accompanied by an adult.

Close season: Open all year.

Disabled Access: Poor/Average. There is a disabled peg with handrails but access to this from the car park is difficult.

Matches: There are a few matches held on the water throughout the year.

Car Parking: There is a car park at the end of Lodge Lane situated at one end of the lodges.

Toilets: None.

Other Facilities: None.

Nearby Amenities: Lostock Tackle Box see address above. Stones Fishing Tackle Shop, 13 Golden Hill Lane, Leyland. Tel: 01772 421953. Open Mon-Tues, Thurs-Fri 9am-5.30pm, Wed 9am-12.30pm, Sat 9am-5pm. Turbary House is the nearest fishery.

Directions: The lodges can be found down Lodge Lane, off Flensburg Way which is part of the A582 Penwortham Way by-pass out of Preston. Lodge Lane is just a short distance from both Croston Road and the local public tip which are both situated between Leyland and Lostock Hall.

FERN GORE

Fern Gore Avenue, Accrington.

A group of three small waters run by the Hyndburn and Blackburn A.A. The first water, which is on your right as you go through the gate, contains a good stamp of roach to over 2lb. The average is quite high with many of the roach caught around the three-quarters of a pound mark. There are tench to 5lb with the average stamp of fish being 2lb. There were some carp in the water but most have been removed and placed in Rishton Reservoir another of the club's waters.

The first water suffered badly from weed growth and so in 1997 the club used a rather unusual method of combating the problem. They placed two garage doors in the water to cover the weed and prevent sunlight reaching it. I can report that the method was a success and that the garage doors are good features to fish to!

The main rectangular shaped water is stocked predominantly with roach and has eight pegs. The third small pond on your left is used as a stock pond.

Cost: The Hyndburn and Blackburn Angling Association club card costs £38 for seniors, £21 for disabled and £13 for juniors and OAP.

Tickets: The club card is available from most East Lancashire tackle shops, see Butts Mill for details.

Rules: One rod only.

Close season: Open all year.

Disabled Access: Good.

Matches: None.

Car Parking: There is space for parking on the concrete bases where some old garages used to stand before they were demolished.

Toilets: None.

Other Facilities: None.

Nearby Amenities: You are close to the centre of Accrington. The Spinning Jenny pub. The nearest tackle shop is Hyndburn Angling Centre, 71 Abbey Street, Accrington. Tel: 01254 397612. Open Mon-Tues 9am-5pm, Wed 9am-12pm, Thurs 9am-5pm, Fri-Sat 9am-5.15pm. Other Hyndburn and Blackburn A.A. waters in the area are Clarendon Street Reservoir, Kerns Allen and Slate Pits.

Directions: The waters can be found on Fern Gore Avenue, off Willows Lane in Accrington.

FIR TREE FISHERY
The Nook, Appley Bridge.

This is the second of two fisheries in the book that are not actually within the current Lancashire boundaries. However, Fir Tree misses out on membership to the Red Rose county by less than quarter of a mile!

The fishery is unique in that it is surrounded by Scots Pine and Norway Spruce. The fishery holds carp to 19lb, tench to 6lb, bream to 3lb, roach to 2lb plus, chub, ghost carp, golden tench, golden orfe, koi and rudd.

The first water, which holds 15 anglers is called the Scots Pine Pond. It has average depths of 5ft and contains a slightly larger stamp of fish than the Blue Spruce Lake.

Blue Spruce Lake has 30 pegs and is slightly deeper with an average depth of 6ft but with areas 10ft deep.

Cost: Summer rates for day tickets are £5 for adults and £3 for OAP, disabled and juniors. Evening tickets are available after 5pm for £3. Winter rates are

£3.50 for a day ticket with an evening ticket available after 3pm for £3. Day tickets permit the use of two rods.

Tickets: Pay on bank.

Rules: Barbless hooks only. No keepnets. No boilies, nuts, trout pellets, cereal baits, breadfeed or groundbait. Hemp in moderation. Landing nets must be dipped before you commence fishing. No under-sixteens unless accompanied by an adult. No night fishing.

Close season: Open all year.

Disabled Access: Good.

Matches: Yes. Club bookings can be taken. Matches will only ever be held on one of the waters at once.

Car Parking: Yes. Behind the house next to Scots Pine Pond.

Toilets: None.

Other Facilities: Snacks such as bacon butties are available at 11am.

Nearby Amenities: The Wheatsheaf pub on Miles Lane and the Waters Edge pub down Mill Lane next to the convenience store both sell food. Nearby fisheries are Beacon View and Charity Farm.

Directions: Leave the M6 at junction 27 and head for the A5209 to Wrightington and Parbold. On leaving the motorway roundabout take an immediate left down Back Lane which is opposite the petrol station. Go to the end of Back Lane and then turn left onto Miles Lane. The fishery is on your left after the convenience store and petrol station. Turn left onto Park Hey Drive and immediately right down The Nook. Follow the track over the little bridge, go to your left past the front of the house and then round the back to the car park.

Contact: For further information contact 01257 252607.

FOULRIDGE (LOWER) RESERVOIR
A56 Skipton New Road, Colne.

Large shoals of bream can make a days angling on this water an arm-aching experience. Pleasure anglers have been known to take bags of fish in excess of 70lb and matches are regularly won with weights into double figures. There are also plenty of roach present and a total of 300 carp which generally weigh between 15lb and 20lb. Perch, tench and pike are other features of the water with pike now reaching over 20lb being caught. The odd trout that has slipped through from the upper reservoir often makes a lively addition to the days captures!

Cost: Day tickets for one rod cost £3.50 for adults and £2.25 for juniors and OAP. A second rod costs half the price of the day ticket.

John Parrott with an 11lb pike from Foulridge Reservoir

Tickets: The day tickets can be obtained on the bank from the bailiff who patrols the water.

Rules: No night fishing unless you are a member of the syndicate. No keepnets between 15th March and 15th June inclusive.

Close season: Open all year.

Disabled Access: Poor.

Matches: To book a match on the water telephone the Pendle Leisure Services on 01282 661230.

Car Parking: There is no designated car park.

Toilets: None.

Other Facilities: None.

Nearby Amenities: Colne. Boyces Fishing Tackle, 44 Manchester Road, Nelson. Tel: 01282 614412. Open Mon-Sat 9am-5pm except Tues 9am-1pm. Ballgrove Lake and Knotts Lane ponds.

Directions: The reservoir can be found to the north of Colne on the A56 to Skipton, which actually passes between the upper and lower reservoirs.

Contact: For further information telephone the Pendle Leisure Services on 01282 661230.

FOUNDRY LODGE
Town Lane, Whittle-le-Woods.

The lodge holds 18 anglers and has an average depth of around 4ft. At the far end the lodge is shallower and is about 2ft.

There are many pike around the 2lb-3lb mark with one specimen reported to be much bigger than all the rest. How much it weighs is a question that may well be best answered by one of the readers of this book, when they catch it!

There are bream to 7lb with an average around 4lb with lots of skimmers too. The tench go to over 6lb and average 3lb plus. There are also roach, rudd, crucian, perch and the odd eel. There are some nice roach in the lodge between half a pound and a pound.

Cost: Day tickets are £2 a rod.

Tickets: Pay on the bank.

Rules: Take litter home. No trout pellets as feed, hookbaits only. Groundbait in moderation. No night fishing. Take care near the overhead power cables. No keepnets between March 15th and June 15th inclusive.

Close season: Open all year.

Disabled Access: Poor/Average.

Matches: None.

Car Parking: To find the car park, go to the back of the foundry and when you reach the end take the track up to your right and then to the left. Beware:- the gates may be locked while you are still on the fishery. To prevent getting your car locked in, check when the gates will be closed. The gates to the foundry will be locked on a Sunday.

Toilets: None.

Other Facilities: None.

Nearby Amenities: The Roebuck pub is opposite Town Lane. Heapey Lodges is the nearest fishery.

Directions: The lodge can be found off Town Lane in Whittle-le-Woods. Taking the A6, Preston Road, out of Chorley, turn right down Shaw Brow just before you reach Shaw Hill Golf Club on your left. When you reach the bottom of Shaw Brow bear right after the post office and then take an immediate right down Town Lane and then a sharp left into the grounds of the foundry. Or, alternatively, you can park your car on the road and take the public footpath to the water which is just after the entrance to the works.

GAWTHORPE HALL POND

Padiham.

The Marsden Star Angling Club runs this water and it can only be fished on their season permit. The pond has room for about eight anglers and holds carp to 16lb, tench to 3lb, roach, perch and the odd skimmer bream. The carp average around 9lb.

Cost: A season permit costs £18 for adults and £9 for juniors.

Tickets: The permit can be obtained from most East Lancashire tackle shops including Boyces Fishing Tackle, 44 Manchester Road, Nelson. Tel: 01282 614412. Open Mon-Sat 9am-5pm except Tues 9am-1pm. Mack's Tackle, 33a Parliament Street, Burnley. BB11 3JU. Tel: 01282 427386. Open Mon-Wed 9am-5.30pm, Thurs 9.30am-6pm, Fri 9am-6pm, Sat 9am-5pm. If you have trouble obtaining the club card, you can write to one of the Membership Secretaries at 3 Duerden Street, Nelson, BB9 9BJ.

Rules: Contained in club card. Includes no night fishing.

Close season: Open all year.

Disabled Access: Poor.

Matches: Club matches, open matches and junior matches are held on the water.

Car Parking: There is a car park on your left as you approach the Hall down the driveway.

Toilets: There are some toilets located in the grounds of the Hall.

Other Facilities: None.

Nearby Amenities: There are shops a couple of minutes away. Lower House Lodge is the nearest fishery.

Directions: Leave the M65 at junction 10 and take the A671 to Padiham. Following the signs for Gawthorpe Hall turn right into the grounds and there is parking on your left as you approach the Hall. Please do not park in front of the Hall or on the approach road, use the designated car parking. To find the water, walk up to the front of the Hall, then up the steps and the hill to reveal the pond.

GREAT BIRCHWOOD
Off A584 Lytham Road, between Warton and Lytham.

This is a caravan and equestrian centre as well as a fishing venue. The complex holds American Line Dancing events and car boots and so can get very busy at weekends. The three ponds hold carp, crucians, tench, bream and roach. The carp run to 27lb in the main pond with several other fish in double figures.

Cost: £10 for a maximum of two rods with no concessions.

Tickets: Day tickets are purchased on the bank.

Rules: Keepnets are not allowed. No boilies.

Close season: Open all year.

Disabled Access: Good.

Matches: None.

Car Parking: Yes. You can park alongside the waters.

Toilets: Yes.

Other Facilities: There is a bar and restaurant open at weekends.

Nearby Amenities: Tavernors Outdoor Pursuits, 33 North Clifton Street, Lytham. Tel: 01253 796182. Open Mon-Sat 9am-5.30pm.

Directions: Directly off the A584 road into Lytham on the right-hand side just before Nevada Bob's golf shop and driving range. A large ranch-style entrance greets you on entry to the complex.

Contact: For more information contact Tony Hadlow on 01772 633162.

GREENHALGH LODGE
Greenhalgh Lane, Esprick near Kirkham.

This carp only water generally holds fish averaging around 8lb but fish up to 18lb have been caught. There are 37 pegs plus one disabled peg and the average depth is around 4ft. The water is geared more to the match and pleasure angler than the carp specialists.

Cost: Day tickets run from 7am until dusk and cost £4.

Tickets: Available on the bank.

Rules: Only one rod can be used at once. Barbless hooks only, of which the smallest size allowed is 14, a minimum hooklength strength of 4lb(no braided hooklengths), no boilies, tiger nuts, peanuts or bloodworm and joker, no groundbait or liquidised bait. Keepnets are not allowed and landing nets must be dipped before you commence fishing. Dogs are also banned.

Close season: Open all year.

Disabled Access: Good.

Matches: The fishery runs matches on Saturday mornings and Thursday evenings.

Car Parking: Yes.

Toilets: Yes. There are toilets and a washroom.

Other Facilities: Plans for a 40-seater cafe.

Nearby Amenities: The Blue Anchor pub. Kirkham Angling Centre, Freckleton Street, Kirkham. Tel: 01772 499252. Open Mon-Sat 9am-5.30pm. Noah's Ark, 41 Lower Green, Poulton-le-Fylde. FY6 7EJ. Tel: 01253 885684. Open Mon-Sat 8am-5.30pm.

Directions: To find the lodge leave junction 3 of the M55 and take the A585 to Fleetwood. About a mile down this road is the Blue Anchor pub and opposite are some white railings and Greenhalgh Lane. Turn down this lane and the fishery is one and a half miles down this road on the left-hand side.

Contact: For further details telephone 01253 836348.

GRIMSARGH RESERVOIRS
Grimsargh.

There are three reservoirs under the control of the Red Scar Angling Club. The first reservoir is for trout fishing and can only be fished by members of the club or on a guest day ticket if accompanied by a club member.

Reservoirs 2 and 3 are for coarse fishing and are available to members and also on a day ticket. The No 2 reservoir holds pike to 26lb, carp to 25lb, tench and bream to 9lb, roach and perch. Reservoir No 3 contains tench, bream, crucians and roach.

Alan Unsworth with a 19lb 2oz pike from Grimsargh Reservoirs

Cost: Day tickets are £4 for adults, £2 for disabled/OAP and £1 for under-six-teens.

Tickets: Available from Ted Carter's, 85-88 Church Street, Preston. Tel: 01772 253476. Open Mon-Sat 9am-5.30pm, closed Thursdays. There is a waiting list of 50 people to join the Red Scar Angling Club. If you wish to put your name on the list write to the Membership Secretary at 14 Old Station Close, Grimsargh, Preston. PR2 5JD.

Rules: A full set of rules is provided with your day ticket but they include no friends to accompany those fishing. No dogs. Fishing after 6am only. No keepnets 15th March to 15th June. No carp in keepnets. Deadbaits and spinning for pike in No 2 only. No coarse fish to be used as deadbait. You must leave the water by 9pm in April, 10pm in May, 11pm in June/July, 10pm in August, 8.30pm in September and sunset for the rest of the months.

Close season: Open all year.

Disabled Access: Good. There are two disabled platforms on reservoir No 3.

Matches: There are 18 matches a year held on No 3 for members only.

Car Parking: There is a car park in front of the middle reservoir. A key to the car park gate can be acquired for a £5 returnable deposit.

Toilets: Yes, including a disabled toilet.

Other Facilities: There is a cabin to allow you to shelter from the rain.

Nearby Amenities: There is a newsagents just past the entrance to the reservoir. Ted Carter's – see address above. Nearby fisheries include Lyndhurst at Longridge and Woodfold and Horns Dam around Goosnargh.

Directions: The reservoirs can be found in the centre of Grimsargh, partly hidden from the road by houses. If you turn off the A5085, Blackpool Road, which runs right through Preston, onto the B6243, Ribbleton Avenue, and then follow this road right through you will reach Grimsargh. On your way, you should pass the Red Scar and Roman Way Industrial Estates and Preston Crematorium. Once in Grimsargh the reservoirs can be found on your left-hand side soon after you have passed the Post Office on your right.

HAGGS RESERVOIR
Off Hyndburn Road, Accrington.

Fishing on this reservoir is controlled by the Accrington and District Fishing Club. The reservoir has around 20 pegs and has an average depth of about 7ft. It is full of carp to 15lb, bream to 4lb, tench, roach and perch.

The stocks were boosted by the introduction of fish from the club's former water Platts Lodge at Victoria Street, Accrington, which has been closed to allow work to be carried out on it.

Cost: Membership to the Accrington and District Fishing Club coarse section is £40 for seniors and £6 for juniors. A night permit which allows you to fish at night with two rods is an extra £30.

Tickets: The club card is available from Leonard's Angling, 5 Whalley Road, Clayton-le-Moors, Accrington. Tel: 01254 231148. Open Mon-Sat 9am-5pm, Sun 8.30am-11.30am. Roe Lee Tackle Box, 336 Whalley New Road, Blackburn. Tel: 01254 676977. Open Mon-Sat 9am-5.30pm. Hyndburn Angling Centre, 71 Abbey Street, Accrington. Tel: 01254 397612. Open Mon-Tues 9am-5pm, Wed 9am-12pm, Thurs 9am-5pm, Fri-Sat 9am-5.15pm.

Rules: One rod during daylight hours. Two rods at night if you have purchased the extended coarse ticket.

Close season: The club operates an alternating close season between the Haggs Reservoir and Rishton Paper Mill. In the 2000 season, the reservoir will be closed between 15th March and 15th June inclusive and, in 2001, Rishton Paper Mill will be closed during the same period.

Disabled Access: Average.

Matches: Club matches only.

Car Parking: There is parking on the Asda car park.

Toilets: None. Although with a bit of discretion, you may be able to use the Asda toilets.

Other Facilities: None.

Nearby Amenities: The reservoir is behind the Asda store and so for food or snacks Asda is the obvious choice. The nearest tackle shop is Hyndburn Angling Centre see address above. The closest fisheries are Clarendon Street Reservoir, Slates Pits and Fern Gore.

Directions: The reservoir can be found close to Asda off the A679, Hyndburn Road, in the centre of Accrington.

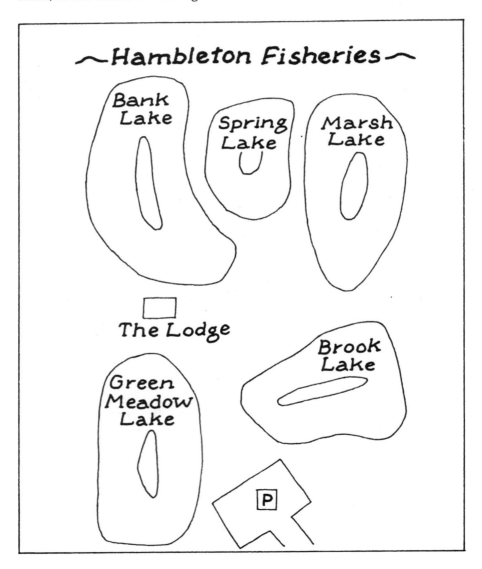

HAMBLETON FISHERIES

Salt Marsh Lane, Hambleton.

This fishery provides anglers with the choice of over 100 pegs spread across five lakes. The lakes were dug in 1996 and they are all around 6 ft deep and everyone has an island to fish to. There are two lakes at one acre and the other three are each around three-quarters of an acre.

The fishing is well spread throughout the lakes. There are carp to 15lb although the average weight of the carp stock is nearer 2lb. There are also barbel, chub, tench, roach and rudd. Most of the fish are around the 1lb mark but with the lakes being relatively new there is much scope for rapid growth weights.

The lakes are surrounded by substantial windbreaks which provide welcome protection from the elements, especially in the colder winter months.

Cost: Day tickets are available for £5. Concessions are £4. An extra rod costs £3. The fishery operates an evening ticket which is £4 for everyone after 5pm.

Tickets: Pay at the ticket office which is the on site Lodge.

Rules: Barbless hooks only. No groundbait. Maximum line strength 4lb. Night fishing by arrangement only.

Close season: Open all year.

Disabled Access: Average.

Matches: There are open matches held on the fishery. The waters are also available for booking for club matches and corporate days.

Car Parking: The car park is at the entrance to the fishery.

Toilets: Yes.

Other Facilities: There is an on site professional bailiff who is always available for advice and information.

Nearby Amenities: There are the Shovels and Shard Inn pubs and Rosies Kitchen Snacks near by, ask the bailiff for details. The nearest tackle shop is Noah's Ark, 41 Lower Green, Poulton-le-Fylde. FY6 7EJ. Tel: 01253 885684. Open Mon-Sat 8am-5.30pm. Some of the nearby fisheries are Hudsons Farm and Briarcroft plus the membership-only Preesall Pits and Bourbles Lakes.

Directions: Leave the M55 at junction 3 and take the A585 towards Fleetwood, following the signs for Fleetwood Freeport. Turn right onto the A588 at a set of traffic lights and go over the Shard Bridge. The fishery is in the centre of Hambleton village opposite the Total garage.

Contact: For further information telephone 01253 700818.

HARDINGS ANGLING SERVICES

Bryning Road, Wrea Green.

There are four small ponds which can accommodate a maximum of about 25 anglers. All the ponds average 4-5ft in depth.

The main pond, pit B has eight pegs and is full of small carp, tench and roach. The largest carp is only just over 5lb and most of the carp, like the tench, are around 1lb. The biggest tench caught was around 4lb. There are also perch, roach, crucians and rudd in pit B.

Pit C has six pegs and is packed full of tench, crucians, rudd and perch. Pit I also has six pegs and it contains the biggest carp with one fish into double figures. There are several other carp over 5lb but most average around the 1lb to 2lb mark. There are lots of small tench and crucians and plenty of rudd.

Pit F is the least fished due to its location and has the least number of pegs. There is only room for five anglers but the pit holds lots of rudd which are easy to catch, tench and crucians.

Cost: Day tickets are £2.10 for adults and £1.10 for OAPs and children. Weekly tickets are £6 and £3.50 respectively.

Tickets: Tickets must be purchased in advance from Tavernors Outdoor Pursuits, 33 North Clifton Street, Lytham. Tel: 01253 796182. Open Mon-Sat 9am-5.30pm. Kirkham Angling Centre, Freckleton Street, Kirkham. Tel: 01772 499252. Open Mon-Sat 9am-5.30pm. Howarth's, 128 Watson Road, Blackpool. Tel: 01253 344016.

A brochure which details each pit and gives directions is available for 50p and is worth purchasing.

Rules: No tents and no litter. Please respect the farmer's land and keep to the paths and do not block the tracks. Night fishing on pits I and C only.

Close season: Open all year.

Disabled Access: Poor.

Matches: None.

Car Parking: Roadside parking alongside pit B, you may go down the track to the other pits and there is room so you can pull onto the verge.

Toilets: None.

Other Facilities: None.

Nearby Amenities: The attractive village of Wrea Green. There is the Grapes Hotel, a lovely village green, a pond and a couple of small shops. Warton and its shops are about half a mile away and there is also the Birley Arms. Tavernors Outdoor Pursuits tackle shop see above.

Directions: Following the A584 Lytham Road from Preston. Turn right at the traffic lights onto Church Road in the centre of Warton and head towards Wrea Green. Passing the Birley Arms on your right, go down Bryning Lane. The pits can be found on the left and the right down this road.

Contact: For further information contact Tim Harding on 01253 725138.

HEAPEY LODGES
Near Chorley.

There are four lodges on this complex open for fishing. Heapey No 1, 2 and 3 can be fished on day ticket or as a member of Wigan and District A.A. Heapey No 6 is reserved for club members only.

Heapey No 1 is particularly noted for its large numbers of carp with plenty of fish into double figures. It is difficult to accurately predict what the largest fish caught so far weighs but it is certainly into upper double figures. Heapey No 1 is also noted for its stocks of other fish and so proves popular with the general coarse angler. There are roach and perch present to 1lb plus, bream and tench to around the 4lb mark and a small number of chub which are rarely caught. Like the other waters on the complex Heapey No 1 is very, very deep and anglers should make sure they have the tackle to cope with the depths before they fish any of the waters.

Heapey No 2 is noted for its big catches of roach and perch. Both species are abundant in this water. There is now a tremendous head of bream following the stocking of fish up to 2lb plus in order to improve the match fishing. There are also a small number of tench with some carp into double figures. Heapey No 2 is only lightly fished for carp and so if the going gets tough on Heapey No 1 it could be worth having a look to see if you can spot any carp on the move.

Heapey No 3 was closed down and drained for repair work several years ago. It was re-stocked and it holds bream to 4lb, tench to 3lb, roach to 1lb plus, chub and perch. It is not as heavily fished as No 1 and 2.

Heapey No 6 is the members-only water and contains bream to 4lb, roach to 1lb plus, roach/bream hybrids to around 2lb, perch and pike to 15lb.

Cost: The Wigan and District A.A. club card costs £16 for adults, £5 for OAP and only £2 for juniors. Day tickets are £2, £1 and 30p respectively.

Tickets: Day tickets for Heapey No 1, 2 and 3 are available on the bank from the patrolling bailiffs. The club card is available from most tackle shops in Lancashire.

Rules: There is a full set of rules in the club card but they include no tin cans containing sweetcorn, luncheon meat etc. to be taken on waters, all carp must be returned immediately, no night fishing except on Heapey No. 1 – west and south banks. If you wish to night fish then you must first obtain a special night permit for £15, details in the club membership book. Adults are restricted to two rods and juniors one rod. No keepnets 15th March-15th June inclusive.

Close season: Open all year.

Disabled Access: Average. Heapey No 6 is the best for disabled access.

Matches: Are held on the field side of Heapey No 2.

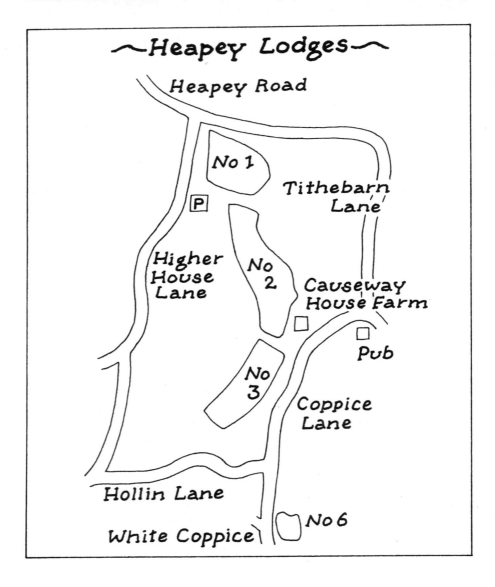

Car Parking: There is a car park overlooking Heapey No 1. There is some parking by Heapey No 6 and this is the best place for disabled anglers.

Toilets: None.

Other Facilities: None.

Directions: The Heapey complex can be found by leaving the M61 at junction 8 and taking the A674 towards Blackburn. A short distance after crossing the canal turn right onto the B6228, Blackburn Road, and follow this road until you see the sign for Heapey and Anglezarke. Turn left here, just before the mini-roundabout, up Knowley Brow, and then follow this road through and it takes you onto Heapey Road. Following the sign for Anglezarke, turn right up Higher House Lane, and about half way up the hill on your left there is a concealed track which takes you to the car park which overlooks Heapey No 1. Alternatively, instead of turning up Higher House Lane, carry on and take a right further along the road at Coppice Lane which is opposite a pub and this will take you nearer to Heapey No 2 and 3.

HESKIN OLD HALL FARM FISHERIES
Halfpenny Lane, Eccleston.

There are three lakes on this farm, which also has room for caravans and camping. Each pond has room for approximately 20 anglers.

Pond No.1 is the place to head for the larger carp. There are fish into the 20lb bracket lurking in the depths of pond No. 1. The lake is 4-7ft deep and holds tench, bream, roach, rudd, perch to 3lb and chub to 2lb alongside the carp.

Pond No. 2 is 7ft deep with spots to 10ft deep. This is probably the most popular pond. There are carp to 15lb, with plenty around the 5-7lb range. Barbel to 4lb, chub, bream, tench, roach and rudd make up the rest of the stock.

Pond No. 3 contains an island and at its deepest is up to 12ft where the original pond was before it was extended. The average depth is 5-6ft and the pond holds carp, ghost koi, tench, golden orfe, roach, rudd, perch and crucians.

Cost: £3 per rod per day. If you fail to pay before commencing fishing you will be asked to pay double on the bank.

Tickets: There is a self-pay system in operation. The pay cabin is on the car park.

Rules: No bloodworm, jokers, breadfeed, trout pellets or boilies. Loosefeed only. Barbless hooks and no keepnets. Nets should be dipped before you commence fishing.

Close season: Open all year.

Disabled Access: There is access to pond No. 2 providing that the field is dry enough to allow you to drive across it.

Matches: Only pond No. 1 and No. 3 are used for matches and not necessarily at the same time. Matches are usually on a Sunday.

Car Parking: There is a large car park which is signposted as you enter the fishery.

Toilets: Yes.

Other Facilities: Caravan Club site and tent spaces.

Nearby Amenities: Eccleston village centre is not far. The Robin Hood pub is near by. There are plenty of other fisheries within a few minutes drive including Barretts, Bluestones and Charity Farm. Tackle and bait can be acquired from Don's Tackle, 8 Mill Street, Coppull. Tel: 01257 794040. Open Mon-Sat 8am-6pm, Sun 8am-1pm.

Directions: To find the fishery follow the signposts for Camelot and Bygone Times and leave the A49, Preston Road, as instructed. Pass Camelot and when you reach the end of Park Hall Road turn right towards the centre of Eccleston. Soon after passing Bygone Times on the left and Pontins headquarters on the right you need to turn left down Bannister Lane. Once you are on Bannister Lane look for a right-hand turning down Halfpenny Lane. Proceed down this narrow and winding road with caution and when you reach the end of it the farm can be found on the right.

HIGH HEYES FARM FISHERY
Eccleston.

This a very attractive 32-peg lake. It is much larger than many of the other fisheries in the immediate area and seems more spacious as you are not as squeezed in. It is also known in the area as 'The Cattery'.

Each peg has some feature in the margins, namely rushes and lilies. There are more lilies out in the lake which are good features to fish to. The bream are a large feature in catches and run to 7lb but there are plenty of skimmer bream. There are carp to 15lb with the species present from weights of 2lb onwards. There are also other species including tench, crucians and perch.

Cost: One rod costs £3.50 per day and two rods are £4.50 per day.

Tickets: There is a self pay system in operation and the pay booth is located on the car park at the entrance to the field leading to the fishery.

Rules: No keepnets, joker or bloodworm. No groundbait and loosefeeding only. No night fishing. Barbless hooks only.

Close season: Open all year.

Disabled Access: Good. Disabled anglers can drive almost up to the water's edge, providing the ground is not too soft. The pegs which are lower to the water are unfortunately at the far end of the lake but can be reached comfortably except in the wettest conditions.

Matches: Competitions are held throughout the year but there is a calendar in the pay booth warning you of the match dates in advance.

Car Parking: Located to your left as you enter the yard.

Toilets: Yes.

Other Facilities: None, unless you wish to purchase dog food or kennel your pet! (If the fishery is busy then it looks as though the farm next door is creating a large lake which could soon be open to coarse fishing and so it may be worth having a look there.)

Nearby Amenities: The centre of Eccleston is very close with the usual shops and pubs. Bygone Times, an antique warehouse, is nearby as is the Camelot Theme Park. Tackle and bait can be acquired from Don's Tackle, 8 Mill Street, Coppull. Tel: 01257 794040. Open Mon-Sat 8am-6pm, Sun 8am-1pm.

Directions: To find the fishery follow the signposts for Camelot and Bygone Times and leave the A49, Preston Road, at Charnock Richard as instructed. Pass Camelot and when you reach the end of Park Hall Road turn right towards the centre of Eccleston. The fishery is on your right before you reach Bygone Times, it is signposted as High Heyes Kennels. Take the dirt track up the hill, bearing left and on reaching the yard bear left again to park.

Contact: For further information contact Merrick Whaite on 01257 450738.

Quality specimens from High Heyes Farm

HIGH ASH LODGE
Wheelton Lane, Leyland.

This lodge provides good sport for a whole variety of coarse species including barbel into double figures! And with tench, bream, roach, rudd, perch, crucian carp and commons and mirrors into double figures you never know what you will catch next. It is run by the Leyland Motors Angling Club and membership runs from 1ˢᵗ January to 31ˢᵗ December. Included in your annual subscription is membership to the Leyland Motors Social Club.

Cost: A season ticket costs adults £20 and senior citizens £10. No under-sixteens can obtain permits for the lodge unless they are also a full member of the Leyland Motors Junior Angling Section.

Tickets: Permits are available from Stones Fishing Tackle Shop, 13 Golden Hill Lane, Leyland. Tel: 01772 421953. Open Mon-Tues, Thurs-Fri 9am-5.30pm, Wed 9am-12.30pm, Sat 9am-5pm.

Rules: No night fishing, groundbait, boilies, trout pellets or paste and barbless or de-barbed hooks only. Keepnets are not allowed between March 15ᵗʰ and June 15ᵗʰ inclusive.

Close season: Open all year.

Disabled Access: Poor.

Car Parking: Roadside parking alongside entrance to fishery.

Toilets: None.

Other Facilities: None.

Nearby Amenities: The centre of Leyland. Stones Fishing Tackle shop, see above.

Directions: The water can be found on Centurion Way at the junction with Wheelton Lane in Leyland.

HODDLESDEN RESERVOIR
Hoddlesden.

The Darwen Loyal Angling Club controls the fishing on this reservoir. You can fish the water on a day ticket but they are limited to five a day. The reservoir contains skimmers, roach to over 2lb, carp to 15lb plus, some good rudd, perch, gudgeon, crucian, tench, a few trout and pike and even the odd goldfish! There are 40 pegs on the reservoir.

Cost: Day tickets are restricted to five a day and cost £2.50.

Tickets: They must be purchased in advance from Geoff Done's Fishing Tackle Shop, 12 Southworth Street, Blackburn. Tel: 01254 698161. Open Mon-Thurs 9am-5.30pm, Fri 9am-6pm, Sat 9am-5pm. There is a waiting list if you wish to join the fishing club.

Rules: You must ALWAYS produce your Environment Agency rod licence when purchasing your day ticket.

Close season: The reservoir is shut for one month – normally May 16th – June 16th. This may vary slightly.

Disabled Access: Average.

Matches: Club matches only.

Car Parking: Yes.

Toilets: None.

Other Facilities: None.

Nearby Amenities: The village of Hoddlesden is only a few minutes away. There are a small number of shops, a chippy and a couple of pubs.

Directions: The reservoir is found alongside the road in the centre of Hoddlesden.

HORNS DAM

Horns Lane, Goosnargh.

The Dam is located within some attractive countryside which provides a tranquil setting to spend a days fishing. The water holds approximately 40 anglers and has depths up to 9ft. It holds some superb tench and bream with both species reaching 7lb in weight. The average size of the fish is also very good and there are plenty of skimmer bream too.

There are carp to 20lb with the fish averaging double figures. Roach, perch, ruffe and eels make up the full complement of species that can be caught from the Dam.

Cost: Day tickets are £4 per person for one rod with an extra rod costing £1.

Tickets: Available on the bank.

Rules: Dip nets before commencing fishing. Barbless hooks only. No peanuts. Under-sixteens must be accompanied by an adult.

Close season: Open all year.

Disabled Access: Poor.

Matches: Matches are held on the Dam. The venue is available to clubs etc who wish to book a match on the water. Warning signs are displayed so that pleasure anglers know a match will be taking place. There is normally room for both pleasure and match anglers even when a club match is being held.

Car Parking: Yes.

Toilets: None.

Other Facilities: The Dam has recently been taken over by new owners who are developing a site alongside the water for 5 Caravan Club member touring caravans with an improved car park.

Alan Yates from Leyland with a 5lb tench from Horns Dam

Nearby Amenities: Goosnargh and Longridge are both about 2 miles away. There are shops in both villages and a chippy at Longridge. Woodfold Farm Fisheries and Lyndhurst Farm Lake are the nearest venues. Just past the Dam are the Ye Horns Inn and the Cottage Inn. There is a touring caravan site behind the Ye Horns Inn.

M.S. Jackson, 33 Moor Lane, Preston. Tel: 01772 558670. Open Mon-Tues, Thurs-Fri 9am-5.30pm, Wed 9am-12pm, Sat 8am-6pm, Sun 6.30am-10.30am (Sundays May-September only).

Directions: Leave the M6 at junction 32 and take the A6 north towards Garstang. Turn right when you reach the Broughton traffic lights at the Golden Ball pub. Follow Whittingham Lane through Goosnargh and past the Stags Head. Where the road takes a sharp right, turn left onto Camforth Hall Lane which means you continue straight on. Keep following this road for quite a distance until you pass the entrance to St Francis's Church and school on your left. The Dam is a short distance past the church on your right before you reach Ford Lane or Ye Horns Inn.

Contact: For further information contact 01772 865239.

HUDSONS FARM
Rawcliffe Road, St Michael's On Wyre.

The fishing on this farm comprises of two small ponds, plus the Doughnut

Lake and the Specimen Lake. The two small ponds can be found close to the track on your way up to the main car park. Both ponds hold chub, roach, rudd, skimmers and perch and one of the ponds has pike to just into double figures.

The Doughnut Lake, which has 18 pegs, has tench to 6lb, chub to 5lb, carp (including ghost carp), bream to 4lb, plenty of skimmers, crucians, roach, rudd, perch and goldfish! The carp run from 6oz to 17lb and the tench and chub both average over two pounds.

The Specimen Lake contains roach, rudd, bream to over 8lb, tench and perch but it is the carp that are of most interest to the anglers fishing this lake. The biggest fish caught so far is a mirror which weighed over 23lb. There are ghost carp to 17lb plus and commons to 19lb plus. The average size of fish currently caught is around the 12lb mark.

Despite the Specimen Lake catching the attention of the carp angler, the pleasure angler should not overlook the lake as it holds some large shoals of skimmer bream.

Cost: Fishing costs £4 per day and this allows you to fish all of the waters and if you wish, you can swap between them. Juniors below 15 and OAPs can fish for £3. A 24-hour ticket costs £7.50 with no concessions.

Tickets: You can either pay at the house before commencing fishing or the bailiff will come round and collect your money.

Rules: Maximum three rods. Keepnets are not allowed. No nut baits e.g. tiger nuts and peanuts, bloodworm and joker or fully barbed hooks. Microbarbed or barbless hooks can be used.

Close season: Open all year.

Disabled Access: Poor.

Matches: Club matches are held on the Doughnut Lake only.

Car Parking: Follow track through the yard and there is parking near the Specimen Lake.

Toilets: Yes.

Other Facilities: The farm is a Caravan Club certified location. Basic snacks may be available.

Nearby Amenities: The shops and the Grapes pub in the centre of St Michael's are about a mile away. Other fisheries in the area include Briarcroft, Toad Hall and Wyreside.

Directions: The lakes can be found a short distance from Briarcroft Fishery. To find the fishery, turn off the A6 in Bilsborrow following the signs for Myerscough College and Guy's Thatched Hamlet. Continue along this road until it ends and then turn right at the mini-roundabout before turning left onto Rawcliffe Road in the centre of the village. Following Rawcliffe Road, you will come to the entrance to Hudsons Farm on your right-hand side.

Contact: For further information contact the bailiff, Tommy Roskell, on 01995 679654.

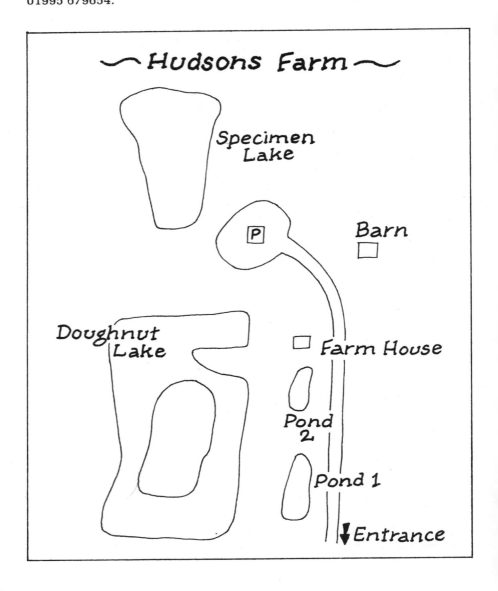

HURLSTON HALL COARSE FISHERY

Off the A570, near Ormskirk.

This lake has only recently been converted from a trout fishery into a coarse venue. There is a carp around the 30lb mark with several others into double figures. There has been a large stocking of carp weighing 1lb and these have already grown fast. Another stocking of carp in the 3lb-6lb bracket is planned. There are also tench to 6lb, chub and lots of roach and rudd.

There are 38 pegs available on this attractive lake which is alongside a well-run caravan site. If you are looking for a place to stay in your touring caravan and fancy a spot of fishing then this site should be near the top of your list.

Cost: Day tickets are £4 for visiting anglers, £3 for caravan residents or those staying on site in a touring van and £1.50 for under-sixteens. Evening tickets are available for £2.50 after 5pm.

Tickets: If you arrive before 9am your money will be collected on the bank otherwise please pay at reception.

Rules: Barbless hooks only. No keepnets. No trout pellets or nuts. Groundbait in moderation only. No pre-baiting. No night fishing. Fishing is from 7am-11.30am. No dogs. No under-sixteens unless accompanied by an adult. Please be quiet when entering and leaving the fishery especially early in a morning or late at night. The lake is for fishermen only, no casual visitors. Please do not feed the wildlife at any time. No litter. The rules may be added to or amended as the fishery is relatively new.

Close season: The lake is closed from the end of October until Easter in line with the caravan season.

Disabled Access: Average.

Matches: None.

Car Parking: Yes. After going up the drive, turn right into the caravan park. Go straight on through the park past the touring bays and there is a large car park near the water.

Toilets: Yes. You need to get the key from reception.

Other Facilities: Caravan site for touring vans. It is £10 per night (including two adults and electrical hook up at £2 a night). Extra adults or children over five years old are £1 a night. There are special offers including seven nights for the price of six and longer-term deals. Laundry room, showers and facilities for the disabled.

Nearby Amenities: Opposite the caravan site is a golf course. Temporary membership, restaurant and bar facilities can be arranged for those staying on the caravan site. The centre of Southport is 10 minutes drive. There are attractions for all the family including the Pleasureland, pitch and putt, putting green, crazy golf, gardens, pier, amusement arcades and shops. White Rails Farm fishery is nearby. The nearest tackle shop is Burscough Angling Supplies, Lords Gate Lane, Burscough. Tel: 01704 896252. Open Mon-Sat 9am -5.30pm.

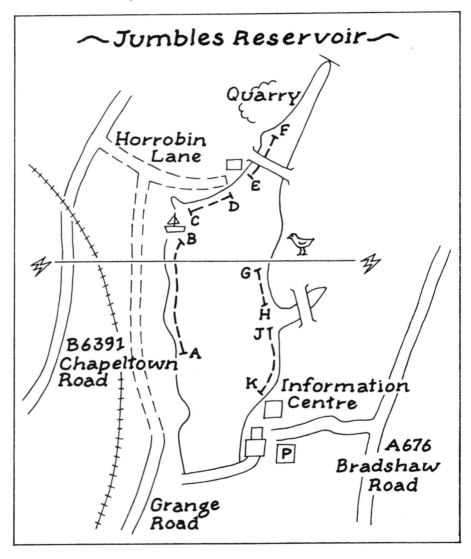

Directions: Follow the A59 from Preston to Liverpool and when you reach the main traffic lights in Ormskirk turn right onto the A570 to Southport. Beware this is a rather awkward junction. The fishery is a short distance down here on the right-hand side shortly after passing Blindmans Lane on your left. The entrance to the fishery is shared with the drive to the Hurlston Hall Golf Club.

Contact: For further information contact Hurlston Hall Country Caravan Park, Southport Road, Scarisbrick, Ormskirk, Near Southport, Lancashire. L40 8HB. Telephone 01704 841064.

JUMBLES RESERVOIR
Off the A676, north of Bolton

The reservoir can be found in the heart of the Jumbles Country Park and provides sport for pike, perch, barbel, tench, bream and roach. There are also brown and rainbow trout present.

Cost: The fishing is free but all anglers must be in possession of an Environment Agency rod licence.

Rules: Fishing is between the areas marked A-B, C-D, E-F, H-G and J-K. Length E-F is for the use of Bolton & District Anglers Association permit holders only. Fishing from sunrise to sunset only. No wading or boat fishing. No under-sixteens unless accompanied by an adult. No live baiting, spinning or fly-fishing. You can obtain a full set of fishing regulations and map from the information centre. The rules and regulations are also displayed on boards around the reservoir.

Close season: The reservoir is closed from 15th March to 15th June inclusive.

Disabled Access: The best disabled access is off the B6391 Chapeltown Road down Horrobin Lane.

Matches: None.

Car Parking: There is ample car parking off the A676 Bradshaw Road which is signposted.

Toilets: Yes.

Other Facilities: There is a Tea Garden which is open Wednesdays and Saturdays in season 1pm-5pm. It is open on Sundays 11am-5pm. There is the Jumbles Information Centre.

Nearby Amenities: There are a whole host of pubs off both the A676 and B6391 including the Lamb, the Bulls Head and the King William.

Directions: From Bolton, take the A676 Bradshaw Road through Bradshaw to Jumbles Reservoir. There are signposts directing you to the car parks and information centre.

Contact: The Jumbles Reservoir Information Centre can be contacted on

01204 853360. Please note the centre is only open for a limited number of hours each week and your call may be diverted to the Rivington Information Centre.

For map, see next page.

JUNIOR LODGE
Off A674 at Withnell Fold.

This lodge is one of two Withnell Anglers' venues that can be found almost alongside one another.

The Junior Lodge provides some quality carp fishing despite there being only 8 pegs. There are carp to over 30lb with the average a respectable 17lb. There are also roach and perch in the lodge for the general coarse angler although the water is predominantly a carp venue. The lodge is also sometimes referred to as Spring Pool.

Cost: Season tickets for Withnell Anglers are £35 for those who live within the parish of Withnell, which includes Abbey Village, Brinscall and Withnell Fold. Those who live outside the parish boundary can join as associate members for £45.

Tickets: To join the club you must apply to the Membership Secretary at PO Box 41, Chorley, PR6 8JZ. For further information contact Membership Secretary Bernard Wren on 01254 830935.

Rules: Club members only, no day tickets. Maximum of two rods. No keepnets in the close season. Maximum stay of 24 hours in any one swim. ALL anglers are responsible for ANY litter found within 10ft of their fishing position.

Close season: Open all year.

Disabled Access: Poor.

Matches: Club matches only.

Car Parking: None. There is room for one car on the lane next to the lodge.

Toilets: None.

Other Facilities: None.

Nearby Amenities: Cricket Field Lodge, Rakes Brook and Roddlesworth, Shale Holes and Croft Lodge are nearby Withnell Anglers' waters. Withnell Fisheries is very close.

Directions: Leave the M65 at junction 3 and at the roundabout take the A674 towards Higher Wheelton. You will soon reach the small village of Withnell Fold. Turn right into the village and follow the track round up to your left towards the cricket field. The lodge is halfway up this track behind the houses and before the Cricket Field Lodge.

KERNS ALLEN
Rising Bridge.

The access to this fishery has improved dramatically following a lot of remedial work. There are two lodges which are controlled by Hyndburn and Blackburn A.A. The first lodge has about 10 pegs and the second about 15 pegs.

They contain a good mix of coarse fish with carp to 20lb, pike to double figures, bream to 5lb plus, tench to 6lb plus, roach and perch.

Cost: The Hyndburn and Blackburn Angling Association club card costs £38 for seniors, £21 for disabled and £13 for juniors and OAP.

Tickets: The club card is available from most East Lancashire tackle shops, see Butts Mill for details.

Rules: One rod only. Two rods are permitted in the hours of darkness. If you are fishing with two rods, at least one must be on an audible alarm.

Close season: Open all year.

Disabled Access: Good. There is a path and platforms around the waters. A bridge has been built over the area that you once had to jump across!

Matches: Club matches only.

Car Parking: There is a gravelled area for parking on.

Toilets: None.

Other Facilities: None.

Nearby Amenities: There is a Little Chef on the main road. Nearest tackle shop is Hyndburn Angling Centre, 71 Abbey Street, Accrington. Tel: 01254 397612. Open Mon-Tues 9am-5pm, Wed 9am-12pm, Thurs 9am-5pm, Fri-Sat 9am-5.15pm. Other Hyndburn and Blackburn A.A. waters in the area are Clarendon Street Reservoir, Fern Gore and Slate Pits.

Directions: The two lodges are at Rising Bridge, which is between Accrington and Haslingden.

KNIGHT BOTTOM LAKE
Green Lane, Samlesbury.

This small lake is only two thirds of an acre but holds carp to 22lb and tench around the 3-4lb mark. There are also roach up to one and a half pounds, perch and rudd in this water which has depths varying from 3-8ft.

The owner wishes to keep the fishing of a high standard and so allows only six anglers per day even though the water could hold up to 20 people.

Cost: Day tickets are £5 for a maximum of two rods. You must book over the phone before your visit.

Tickets: Pay at the house unless it is early morning and then your money will be collected on the bank.

Rules: Rules include barbless hooks only, no nuts or pulses and no keepnets. Minimum line strength of 5lb. No night fishing. Fishing is from 7am.

Close season: Open all year.

Disabled Access: Average.

Matches: Some matches are fished on the lake but these are rare due to only six pegs being available.

Car Parking: Yes.

Toilets: Yes.

Other Facilities: None.

Nearby Amenities: Blue Slate and Red Rocks Fisheries. Samlesbury Hall.

Directions: To find the lake leave the M6 at junction 31(Tickled Trout) and head up the A59 towards Blackburn. When you reach Samlesbury Hall, turn right down Nabs Head Lane. After you have passed the Nabs Head pub turn right again down Goosefoot Lane and then on the brow of a hill take another right turn into Green Lane. The lake is about half a mile down here on the right-hand side. You need to turn right through the big green gates and follow the track down to the farm.

Contact: For further information and to book call 01254 852206.

KNOTTS LANE PONDS
Knotts Lane, Colne.

These two ponds are run by the Marsden Star Angling Club and can be fished on a day ticket or as a club member.

Each pond holds approximately 10 anglers and contains carp to 25lb, bream to 6lb, tench to 4lb, roach and perch. The carp average into double figures.

Cost: Day tickets are limited to three per day and are £3. A season permit costs £18 for adults and £9 for juniors.

Tickets: Day tickets are available on the bank. The season permit can be obtained from most East Lancashire tackle shops including Boyces Fishing Tackle, 44 Manchester Road, Nelson. Tel: 01282 614412. Open Mon-Sat 9am-5pm except Tues 9am-1pm. Mack's Tackle, 33a Parliament Street, Burnley. BB11 3JU. Tel: 01282 427386. Open Mon-Wed 9am-5.30pm, Thurs 9.30am-6pm, Fri 9am-6pm, Sat 9am-5pm. If you have trouble obtaining the club card, you can write to one of the Membership Secretaries at 3 Duerden Street, Nelson, BB9 9BJ.

Rules: Contained in club card. Includes no night fishing.

Close season: Open all year.

Disabled Access: Poor.

Matches: None.

Car Parking: Roadside parking only.

Toilets: None.

Other Facilities: None.

Nearby Amenities: Foulridge Reservoir and Ballgrove Lake are the nearest fisheries. There is a convenience store and off-licence at the bottom of the hill on Knotts Lane.

Directions: Follow the M65 until it ends at Colne and then turn right at the roundabout onto the A6068, Whitewalls Drive. At the next roundabout, turn left onto the A56 towards the centre of Colne. After passing under the railway, turn right into Bridge Street. This leads into Knotts Lane and the ponds are on your left.

LANCASTER CANAL

The canal starts in the centre of Preston, just off Fylde Road, and it is here that some of the best fishing can be found. However, in fairness, you can find plenty of fish to be caught throughout the length of the canal right up to Lancaster, Morecambe and beyond.

The canal holds most coarse fish with roach in abundance, bream, tench, rudd, ruffe, perch, gudgeon and the small bitterling. There are always a few eels to be found up and down the canal but I think that most anglers try to avoid them rather than catch them. (Unless they are in a match!)

The roach rarely grow bigger than a pound and if you can locate a shoal of fish of half a pound plus then you should enjoy your days fishing.

There are plenty of skimmer bream and although most do not grow much bigger than 2lb you can find some shoals of bream between 4lb-6lb. If you are lucky enough to locate a shoal of bream this size then it is not unheard of to make a catch topping the magical ton mark although these captures are rare and often come when the bream have shoaled up for winter or spawning.

The pike are mainly single figure fish and, with miles of canal and plenty of small fish as prey, they are rarely caught, although that may be because I have only seen a small number of pike anglers on the canal.

Matches can be won with double-figure bags, but most winning weights are normally around 3lb-4lb. However, pleasure anglers, if they pick the right area and fish well, can expect double figure captures and on a special day could net over 50lb of fish.

Location really is the key. There are some favoured areas that always produce fish, but with miles of unfished areas, the fish can shoal up for days

without encountering an angler's hookbait. You can find plenty of features
to fish to. Bridges, boat moorings, alongside or opposite boats, overhanging
trees, lily pads, rushes and reeds can all be found on the canal somewhere.
So, too, can wides and basins. These can often provide the best sport but do
not always overlook the normal lengths of canal as this could be to your det-
riment.

You could fish a swim every day for a year and still have a good few years
fishing to try them all. Even then, you have to pick the right swim on the
right day to get a result!

The Ingol area of Preston at Bexhill Road is a good place to start. Or try Shel-
ley Road, Preston, which runs parallel to the canal, where it ends near the
Lane Ends.

Further up at Salwick near the Hand and Dagger pub is another favoured
haunt. The Salwick main basin is in this area and is a particular hotspot.

There are plenty of nice areas all the way up the A6 and it really is up to you
to fish them and find out. There are a couple of good spots at Garstang and
further up near Scorton. At Lancaster, the boatyard can provide some hot
catches in wintertime as too can the boatyard in Carnforth. Apparently, both
areas can throw up 100lb plus of fish, mainly big bream.

There are some grass carp in the stretch above Tewitfield where the canal
was severed so that the M6 motorway could be built. The stretch was closed
for some years while the Lancaster University conducted tests on weed
growth with the grass carp. Left to their own devices they have grown into
some hefty specimens.

There is no boat traffic on this stretch and so the rushes and reeds have
grown halfway across the canal in some parts. The length can be located behind the Burton services on the M6.

Cost: The Lancaster Canal is part of the British Waterways Wanderers
(BWW) scheme. They control the entire 55 miles of the canal. However, this
means that if your club, such as Preston Centre, Wigan and District A.A.,
Northern Anglers, Lansil, Hyndburn and Blackburn, or Marsden Star are
members of the scheme (denoted by a BWW sticker on your club card) then
you can fish for free. The details of the clubs are listed throughout this book.
The best way is to enquire as to whether your local club is part of the BWW
scheme and if so join them. You then have fishing on the club waters, the
Lancaster Canal and other canals within the scheme including, the
Leeds-Liverpool Canal.

The cheapest club card I know of is Castletown Anglers which simply has
rights to fish the Lancaster Canal and therefore, all the stretches on other canals under the BWW scheme. It is £8 for adults and £4 for juniors and OAP.

The BWW permit is £15 a year for adults and £7.50 junior, OAP and dis-

The Lancaster Canal at Bexhill Road, Preston

abled. Day and monthly tickets can also be purchased for £2/£1.50 and £10/£5 respectively.

The BWW scheme is complex and so it may be a good idea to enquire at your local tackle shop as they often have a sheet with the areas you can fish on each canal under the scheme.

Tickets: Club cards are available from most Lancashire tackle shops or direct. The Castletown card can be obtained from Ted Carter's – see address below.

The BWW permits and further information can be obtained from John Harding 34 Nantwich Road, Tarporley. Cheshire. CW6 9UW. Tel: 01829 732748. Steve Griffiths, Regional Fisheries Manager, British Waterways North West, Navigation Road, Northwich, Cheshire. CW8 1BH. Tel: 01606 74321.

Close season: Open all year.

Useful Contacts: Ted Carter's, 85-88 Church Street, Preston. Tel: 01772 253476. Open Mon-Sat 9am-5.30pm, closed Thursdays. M.S. Jackson, 33 Moor Lane, Preston. Tel: 01772 558670. Open Mon-Tues, Thurs-Fri 9am-5.30pm, Wed 9am-12pm, Sat 8am-6pm, Sun 6.30am-10.30am (Sundays May-September only).

Charlton and Bagnall, 3/5 Damside Street, Lancaster. Tel: 01524 63043. Open Mon-Fri 9am-5.30pm, Sat 9am-5pm, Sun 9.30am-12.30pm. Stephen Fawcett, 7 Great John Street, Lancaster. Tel: 01524 32033. Open Mon-Sat 9am-5pm. Closed Wednesdays.

LANCASTER HOUSE FARM FISHERY
A49, Wigan Road, Charnock Richard.

If you are as afraid of dogs as I am then proceed to this water with caution. When you go to pay at the house, you will find out that the owners have a massive dog which probably weighs more than I do!

The lake itself is a pleasant day ticket fishery which is open dawn until dusk and has a 15 pegs. It is around 5-6ft deep but is up to 8ft deep in places. There are carp to 21lb with others in double figures. Bream, tench, roach, perch, gudgeon and golden orfe are also present.

Cost: £3 for adults and £2 for under-sixteens.

Tickets: Pay at house before commencing fishing.

Rules: No bloodworm, joker, breadfeed or boilies and barbless hooks only. Nets must be dipped before you commence fishing and no keepnets are allowed except in matches. The owners also recommend that under-sixteens are supervised.

Close season: Open all year.

Disabled Access: Good.

Matches: Matches are regularly held on the water at weekends.

Car Parking: As you enter the courtyard turn right between the farm house and farm buildings.

Toilets: Yes.

Other Facilities: None.

Nearby Amenities: There are plenty of other fisheries in the area if the water is busy. They include High Heyes Farm and Old House Farm. Camelot is near. Tackle and bait can be acquired from Don's Tackle, 8 Mill Street, Coppull. Tel: 01257 794040. Open Mon-Sat 8am-6pm, Sun 8am-1pm.

Directions: To find the fishery take the A49, Wigan Road, past Leyland and through Euxton. The entrance to the farm can be found on your right-hand side, opposite Charnock Richard golf course, just before the turn off for Camelot.

Contact: For further details contact Mr Heaton on 01257 791312.

LANGWOOD FARM LODGE
Haslingden Road, Haslingden.

This small lodge has room for only 10 anglers but provides good sport for tench, bream, roach, crucian and perch. The tench and bream have reached top weights of around 6lb and average around the 1lb mark.

The lodge is deep for its size and therefore can hold a good head of quality fish. It is about 5ft in the margins and reaches depths of 13ft in the middle. There are some huge perch to two and a half pound and roach and crucians to a pound and a half.

Cost: Fishing costs £25 for adults and £15 for under-sixteens and OAP for a season ticket and £4 for adults and £2 concessions for a day ticket.

Tickets: There are a limited number of day tickets and these must be booked in advance. Day tickets can be paid for on the bank.

Rules: Barbless hooks only, no groundbait, only one rod to be used at once and fish over 2lb to be returned immediately. No night fishing.

Close season: 15ᵗʰ March-15ᵗʰ June.

Disabled Access: Poor. Unless it is weekends/evenings (See below).

Matches: None.

Car Parking: You have to park on the road which overlooks the lodge but at weekends and evenings you can park on the school grounds allowing easier access to the lodge.

Toilets: None.

Other Facilities: None.

Nearby Amenities: The centre of Rawtenstall is a 2 minute drive or 10 minute walk. Hyndburn Angling Centre, 71 Abbey Street, Accrington. Tel: 01254 397612. Open Mon-Tues 9am-5pm, Wed 9am-12pm, Thurs 9am-5pm, Fri-Sat 9am-5.15pm.

Directions: The lodge is located in Haslingden very close to the Rossendale General Hospital. Take the main A680 through the town and then, at a set of traffic lights, turn onto Haslingden Road. Follow the signs for the hospital, and you will find the entrance down to the lodge on your right-hand side, after a bus stop and just before the All Saints High School and the hospital.

Contact: For more information and to book day tickets telephone Michael between 9am and 5pm on 01706 218300 or 0850 339894.

LATHOM FISHERIES
Warpers Moss Lane, Burscough.

This is a nice lake of 30 pegs which is well stocked according to the regulars. It is around 6ft deep with depths up to 8ft around the island. The lake contains carp to 14lb, tench to around 3lb, roach, rudd, chub, bream, perch, gudgeon, crucians and koi. Fishing is allowed between dawn and dusk.

Cost: £3 a day for adults and £2 for OAP, under-sixteens and disabled.

Tickets: Self pay system in operation.

Rules: No trout pellets, groundbait, breadfeed, bloodworm and joker or boilies. Loosefeed only. No keepnets or night fishing. Barbless hooks only. Anglers are reminded that they must dip nets before commencing fishing. Under-eighteens must be accompanied by an adult.

Close season: Open all year.

Disabled Access: Excellent. You can drive right to your peg and the ground is flat. There are no high banks.

Matches: There are matches held on the water but warning signs are put up in advance.

Car Parking: Car park at entrance to fishery.

Toilets: None.

Other Facilities: None. Although a bailiff will normally be around to offer advice and assistance.

Nearby Amenities: The centre of Burscough and its shops are not far. Ray Wright can provide advice, tackle and bait at Burscough Angling Supplies, Lords Gate Lane, Burscough. 01704 896252. Open Mon-Sat 9am-5.30pm. Platts Lane Lake, Hurlston Hall and White Rails Farm are other fisheries in the area.

Directions: Follow the A59 from Preston to Liverpool passing Rufford Old Hall. Just before you reach the centre of Burscough take the turning on your left, Warpers Moss Lane. If you reach the railway station and the mini roundabout before you have turned left you have gone too far. The fishery is quite a distance down Warpers Moss Lane soon after you have passed under the railway bridge. After a sharp right bend in the road the entrance to the fishery is on your right.

Contact: For further information contact John Morton on 01704 893 914 or 0411 508254.

LEEDS-LIVERPOOL CANAL

The Leeds-Liverpool Canal enters Lancashire from the Merseyside area south-west of Ormskirk. It is here at Halsall, that we shall follow its path through Lancashire until it enters Yorkshire just north of Barnoldswick.

The Wigan and District Anglers Association controls 23 miles of the canal which starts at the Saracens Head in Halsall and ends at the bottom lock at Moss Lane in Chorley. The western end around Halsall is particularly noted for its bream, tench and roach. The canal slips out of Lancashire again as it passes through Wigan and in this area the roach are the predominant species. As the canal passes through Chorley the large bags of bream, tench and roach are not as common as the canal takes on a different character.

The British Waterways control 45 miles of the Leeds-Liverpool Canal and their main length through Lancashire runs from Blackburn to Burnley. The British Waterways Wanderers scheme allows participating clubs to fish their lengths. This means vast lengths of canal are available to a large number of anglers.

The British Waterways length around Rishton and Clayton has been re-stocked on several occasions in recent years. This has improved the fishing on this length and the Hyndburn and Blackburn A.A. often find their open matches are won with nets of roach, perch and skimmers nearing double figures.

The Marsden Star Angling Club has a superb stretch around Barnoldswick. The length has thrown up bags of bream to over 100lb and is a regular on their match calendar. The length runs for a mile from the Salterforth New Road Bridge through Barnoldswick. A particular hotspot is around the Anchor Inn. The club also controls 10 miles of canal at Keighley in Yorkshire.

The Leeds-Liverpool is typical of most northern canals. It can leave you scratching for 'bits' only producing small roach and perch and then another day reward you with a good bag of skimmers and quality bream. Local knowledge seems essential in locating the hotspots.

The canal holds the normal stock of fish you would expect with tench, bream, roach, perch, gudgeon, ruffe and pike with the odd chub and carp.

Cost: The British Waterways control 45 miles of the Leeds-Liverpool canal under their British Waterways Wanderers (BWW) scheme. However, this

The Leeds-Liverpool Canal

means that if your club – such as Preston Centre, Wigan and District A.A., Northern Anglers, Lansil, Hyndburn and Blackburn or Marsden Star are members of the scheme (denoted by a BWW sticker on your club card) then you can fish for free on their lengths. The details of the clubs are listed throughout this book. The best way is to enquire as to whether your local club is part of the BWW scheme and if so join them. You then have fishing on the club waters, this canal and other canals within the scheme, including the entire length of the Lancaster Canal.

The cheapest club card I know of is Castletown Anglers which simply has rights to fish the Lancaster Canal and therefore, all the stretches on other canals under the BWW scheme. It is £8 for adults and £4 for juniors and OAP.

The BWW permit is £15 a year for adults and £7.50 junior, OAP and disabled. Day and monthly tickets can also be purchased for £2/£1.50 and £10/£5 respectively.

The BWW scheme is complex and so it may be a good idea to enquire at your local tackle shop as they often have a sheet with the areas you can fish on each canal under the scheme.

The Wigan and District A.A. club card costs £16 for adults, £5 for OAP and only £2 for juniors.

A season permit for Marsden Star costs £18 for adults and £9 for juniors.

Tickets: The BWW permits and further information can be obtained from John Harding 34 Nantwich Road, Tarporley. Cheshire. CW6 9UW. Tel: 01829 732748. Steve Griffiths, Regional Fisheries Manager, British Waterways North West, Navigation Road, Northwich, Cheshire. CW8 1BH. Tel: 01606 74321.

The Marsden Star permit can be obtained from most East Lancashire tackle shops including Boyces Fishing Tackle, 44 Manchester Road, Nelson. Tel: 01282 614412. Open Mon-Sat 9am-5pm except Tues 9am-1pm. Mack's Tackle, 33a Parliament Street, Burnley. BB11 3JU. Tel: 01282 427386. Open Mon-Wed 9am-5.30pm, Thurs 9.30am-6pm, Fri 9am-6pm, Sat 9am-5pm. If you have trouble obtaining the club card you can write to one of the Membership Secretaries at 3 Duerden Street, Nelson, BB9 9BJ.

The Castletown card can be obtained from Ted Carter's, 85-88 Church Street, Preston. Tel: 01772 253476. Open Mon-Sat 9am-5.30pm, closed Thursdays.

The Wigan and District A.A. club card and other club cards who are members of the BWW scheme can be obtained from most Lancashire tackle shops.

Close season: Open all year.

LITTLEDALE FISHERY

Littledale Hall, Near Caton.

This picturesque little fishery has 15 pegs and is full of carp to over 20lb, with most of the fish averaging in double figures. There are both common and mirror carp, quality roach to 2lb plus, tench and bream to 3lb and perch.

Cost: Day tickets are £3 during the week and £4 at weekends.

Tickets: Must be purchased beforehand from Morecambe Angling Centre, Grand Garage, Thornton Road, Morecambe. Tel: 01524 832332. Open every day including Bank Holidays (except Christmas Day, Boxing Day and New Years Day) Mon-Sat 9am-5.30pm, Sun 9am-12pm.

Rules: No groundbait. Boilies allowed in limited numbers only. Carp over 3lb not to be retained in keepnets. No night fishing.

Close season: Open all year.

Disabled Access: Poor.

Matches: Matches can be booked on the water through the tackle shop.

Car Parking: Small car park near fishery.

Toilets: None.

Other Facilities: None.

Directions: Instructions on how to find the water can be obtained from the tackle shop when purchasing your day ticket.

LONGTON BRICKCROFT

Liverpool Road, Longton.

This water is run by Longton and District Angling Society and can be found off the A59 Preston to Southport by-pass. There are a few lakes on the site but only the lake nearest to the car park and visitor centre is open for fishing. The lakes are former brick pits and depths vary due to the excavations. The depths on the lake range mainly from 4ft-9ft. There are 26 pegs on the water.

The lake holds some quality crucian carp to 3lb, as well as roach, rudd, pike to 9lb plus, bream to 4lb, tench to 6lb, perch, chub, eels to 3lb and carp into double figures with the largest recorded going 15lb 12oz. The local tackle shop (see details below) holds the records for the weights of all the fish. If you catch a larger specimen than the current best and get it verified by two people you may be able to see your achievement recorded for all to see.

Cost: Day tickets are £4 for adults and £1 for juniors and OAP. For two rods it costs £6 and £1.50 respectively. Day tickets are not available on Sundays as it is members only. Membership to the Longton and District Angling Society is available and is reasonably priced. For details contact Tropical Marine Aquatic and Angling Centre see below.

Tickets: Must be bought in advance from Tropical Marine Aquatic and Angling Centre, 73 Liverpool Old Road, Walmer Bridge. Telephone 01772 612941. Fax 01772 619699. Open Mon and Sat 8.30am-5pm, Tues-Fri 8.30am-7pm, Sun 8.30am-4pm. The shop is just a few minutes drive from the water. Full membership to the club also entitles you to a discount at the tackle shop.

Rules: Sunday is members only. Night fishing for members only. Maximum of two rods. No keepnets to be used by day ticket anglers.

Close season: There is a close season from the 16th March to the beginning of June for members and working parties. Day tickets are not available between 16th March and 16th June.

Disabled Access: Good. The car park is close to the water with several pegs nearby. However disabled anglers may be limited to a small choice of pegs.

Matches: Club matches are held on the first Saturday and Sunday of every month and every other Wednesday. Signs are displayed in advance warning of the matches.

Car Parking: On site car parking.

Toilets: Yes. Only available if the Visitor Centre is open.

Other Facilities: None.

Nearby Amenities: There is a bakery opposite the entrance which sells pies and butties. A couple of minutes to your left is Walmer Bridge which has a chippy, pub and pizza place as well as the Tropical Marine Aquatic and Angling Centre see above. To your right is Longton which has several nice pubs which serve food, a chippy and shops.

Turbary House is probably the nearest fishery. There has been some talk of a new water in Much Hoole opening, enquire at the local tackle shop for further details.

Directions: Found off the A59 Preston to Southport by-pass. Following the A59 out of Preston through Penwortham and Hutton when you come to the roundabout with a Little Chef on it follow the signposts to the Longton Brickcroft Nature Reserve.

LOVE CLOUGH
Commercial Street, Love Clough.

The Love Clough Angling Club have access to two ponds which both have room for about 20 anglers each.

The two ponds have roughly the same stock of fish with carp to double figures, tench to 4lb plus, bream, roach and perch. The top pond is slightly deeper, with the hillside end going down to 14ft and the neck end a shallower 4ft. The bottom pond is between 11ft and 4ft.

Cost: Season tickets which allow the use of two rods are £25 for seniors and £7.50 for juniors.

Tickets: To become a member of the Love Clough Angling Club write to the Membership Secretary at 8 Carr Mount, Rawtenstall, Lancashire. BB4 6DF. The membership is restricted to 100 anglers. The club is nearly full and a waiting list is put into operation when the club has 100 members. The club produces a newsletter each year for its members.

Rules: No carp to be retained in keepnets. No keepnets on the bottom pond. Barbless hooks only. No night fishing.

Close season: There is a close season between 28th February and 1st May.

Disabled Access: Poor.

Matches: The club hold matches on the venue for its members.

Car Parking: None. The best place to park is on Manchester Road and then to walk across the field to the water.

Toilets: None.

Other Facilities: None.

Nearby Amenities: The nearest tackle shop is in Burnley. It is Mack's Tackle, 33a Parliament Street, Burnley. BB11 3JU. Tel: 01282 427386. Open Mon-Wed 9am-5.30pm, Thurs 9.30am-6pm, Fri 9am-6pm, Sat 9am-5pm. Penny Lodge can also be found down Commercial Street and Clowbridge Reservoir is about a mile away. The Glory pub on the corner of Commercial

Street and the A682 sells food. There is a shop half a mile down the road if you turn right out of Commercial Street that sells hot food and snacks.

Directions: To find the waters take the A682, Burnley Road, through Love Clough and turn down Commercial Street, then take your next right.

LOWER HOUSE LODGE
Lowerhouse Lane, Padiham.

This is one of the waters run by Pendle and District Anglers Association and it provides fishing for carp to 25lb, pike to 18lb, bream to around 9lb, perch, roach and ruffe. There are plenty of skimmers present in the lodge.

Cost: Day tickets are £2 for adults and £1 for juniors, OAP and disabled. Season tickets are £12 for one rod with an extra rod costing an additional £8.

Tickets: Day tickets are available on the bank and season tickets can be purchased from Mack's Tackle, 33a Parliament Street, Burnley. BB11 3JU. Tel: 01282 427386. Open Mon-Wed 9am-5.30pm, Thurs 9.30am-6pm, Fri 9am-6pm, Sat 9am-5pm. Hyndburn Angling Centre, 71 Abbey Street, Accrington. Tel: 01254 397612. Open Mon-Tues 9am-5pm, Wed 9am-12pm, Thurs 9am-5pm, Fri-Sat 9am-5.15pm.

Rules: Contained on the club card.

Close season: Open all year.

Disabled Access: Poor.

Matches: There are a small number of matches held on the lake.

Toilets: None.

Other Facilities: None.

Directions: The lodge can be found by either turning onto Scott Street off the A671, Burnley to Padiham Road, or taking Lowerhouse Lane off the A646, opposite Lowerhouse County Junior School. The lodge runs parallel to Lowerhouse Lane and is very close to the road on Knotts Lane.

RIVER LUNE

The River Lune flows through the most northern part of Lancashire, which by its very nature, is similar to the terrain found in the Lake District. This means that the river is more suited to the game angler. In fact, the Lune starts its life in Cumbria before flowing over the Lancashire boundary just south of Kirby Lonsdale before making its way to the sea through the centre of Lancaster.

There are only a few stretches of river that will interest the coarse angler. The main stretch is that run by the Lansil Angling Club which can only be fished by its members. Their stretch runs for a mile and a quarter between Howgill

Brook and Deny Beck. Or to locate it by more visual landmarks: from just below the aqueduct at the Lansil industrial estate, which can be found as you enter Lancaster from junction 34 the M6, to upstream of where the M6 crosses the Lune at just below the bridge that takes you over the Lune into Halton.

The Lansil stretch is deep and slow moving but it is definitely the best bet for the coarse angler. The river can be up to 25ft deep in places with an average depth of around 15ft. The river can produce some quality specimens.

There are bream into double figures and the captor of a 4lb roach was lucky enough to have his capture verified by the Environment Agency. The bream average 8lb in weight and can provide some fantastic fishing if you can locate one of the shoals. The roach average over half a pound with the occasional fish topping the 2lb mark. There are also dace to nearly a pound, perch to 4lb, hybrids, gudgeon and ruffe. There are some pike but it is rare to see any caught.

Despite the abundance of coarse fish the Lune can sometimes be erratic and it is those who fish regularly on the river and know its moods that can often produce the best results.

The Lansil stretch is also home to salmon and sea trout in the correct season and the club provide a game permit for anglers who wish to pursue those.

The other two coarse stretches are available on day ticket and are run by the Environment Agency. The first stretch is at Skerton Weir on the outskirts of Lancaster downstream of the Lansil stretch. The second stretch is at Halton on the Halton Top Beat which is more noted for its game fishing. It extends up to the 'Crook O Lune' bridge near Caton. Full details of the permitted fishing areas are on the day ticket and marker posts are on the river bank.

Cost: Membership to the Lansil Angling Club Coarse Fishing Section is £27 for adults, £13 for OAP and £6 for juniors. Membership to the Game section is £60 with a £30 joining fee, no concessions.

The Environment Agency day ticket stretches are £4.

Tickets: To join the Lansil Angling Club you must apply in writing to Lansil Sports and Social Club, Angling Section, Caton Road, Lancaster.

Day tickets can be obtained from Mr Robinson's Newsagents, 6 Sycamore Road, Brookhouse, Lancaster. Tel: 01524 770544. Open Mon-Sat 6am-6pm, Sun 6am-1pm. (The newsagents can be found just through Caton on the left off Brookhouse Road.)

Day tickets are restricted to 24 anglers on the Skerton stretch and 10 on the Halton Top Beat except between 1st Nov-31st Jan when 30 are available.

For any queries regarding day tickets or fishing on the Environment Agency stretches you can contact their fisheries department on 01772 339882.

Close season: The river is closed 15th March to 15th June inclusive.

Useful Contacts: Charlton and Bagnall, 3/5 Damside Street, Lancaster. Tel: 01524 63043. Open Mon-Fri 9am-5.30pm, Sat 9am-5pm, Sun 9.30am-12.30pm. Stephen Fawcett, 7 Great John Street, Lancaster. Tel: 01524 32033. Open Mon-Sat 9am-5pm. Closed Wednesdays.

LYNDHURST FARM LAKE
Halfpenny Lane, Longridge.

This two acre lake can hold a few surprises for the general coarse angler as it contains catfish up to 12lb in weight. There are also carp to 16lb, tench averaging 2lb, bream, roach, rudd and some perch.

Cost: Day tickets are £3 and juniors accompanied by an adult are half price.

Tickets: Available on the bank.

Rules: No night fishing. Barbless hooks only. Groundbait in moderation. No bloodworm or joker. Please dip nets before commencing fishing.

Close season: Open all year.

Disabled Access: Good. You can drive your car close to the pegs.

Matches: Yes.

Car Parking: Car park off Halfpenny Lane in Longridge.

Toilets: None.

Other Facilities: None.

Nearby Amenities: Alston Arms pub. Longridge, which is only a few minutes away, has a chippy and shops. Nearest tackle shop is M.S. Jackson, 33 Moor Lane, Preston. Tel: 01772 558670. Open Mon-Tues, Thurs-Fri 9am-5.30pm, Wed 9am-12pm, Sat 8am-6pm, Sun 6.30am-10.30am (Sundays May-September only).

Directions: If you go through Longridge towards Chipping you need to turn left off Inglewhite Road onto Halfpenny Lane after the Alston Arms pub. The car park can be found on the right-hand side.

Contact: For further information telephone 01772 786420.

McGREALS LODGE
Mill Hill Lane, Hapton, near Padiham.

This lodge is run by the Blackburn and Nalgo Fishing Club and has 12 pegs. The 12ft deep lodge holds carp, bream to 2lb, roach, perch and a few golden rudd.

Cost: Membership to the Blackburn and Nalgo Fishing Club for coarse fishing only is a £15 joining fee and £15 per year. The club also controls some trout waters. Full membership costs £110 per season with an initial joining fee of £30.

Tickets: Information and membership details can be obtained from Mr Maddison, 42 Observatory Road, Blackburn. Tel: 01254 53695.

Rules: No night fishing. Barbless hooks preferred. No day ticket anglers unless accompanied by a member and you have pre-arranged your visit.

Close season: Open all year.

Disabled Access: Average.

Matches: The club hold 5 matches a year on the lodge.

Car Parking: Yes.

Toilets: None.

Other Facilities: None.

Nearby Amenities: The nearest shops are in Hapton village. Lowerhouse Lodge is the nearest fishery. The local tackle shops are Mack's Tackle, 33a Parliament Street, Burnley. BB11 3JU. Tel: 01282 427386. Open Mon-Wed 9am-5.30pm, Thurs 9.30am-6pm, Fri 9am-6pm, Sat 9am-5pm. Leonard's Angling, 5 Whalley Road, Clayton-le-Moors, Accrington. Tel: 01254 231148. Open Mon-Sat 9am-5pm, Sun 8.30am-11.30am.

Directions: The lodge is located in Hapton, which is south of Padiham, off Mill Hill Lane close to Mill Hill Farm.

MANOR HOUSE FISHERIES
Hoole Lane, Nateby, near Garstang.

The three ponds which make up this venue provide good quality fishing for carp to 19lb, tench to 8lb, chub to 6lb plus, bream, roach, rudd and perch.

Pond 1 has 30 pegs and depths to 11ft. Pond 2 is the deepest with depths of 14ft and holds six anglers and Pond 3 is up to 12ft deep and has 12 pegs. As well as the usual commons, mirrors and crucian carp there has also been some ghost carp stocked.

The ponds contain some monster perch with the biggest recorded so far weighing in excess of 3lb 12ozs. Winter time consistently produces captures of perch in the 2lb to 3lb bracket from Ponds 2 and 3.

Although the fishery is still a day ticket water the management have introduced a membership scheme to protect the fishery and its anglers. To be able to fish the waters you must have a private recommendation from either a local tackle shop or be able to a provide a suitable reference for yourself. Once you have fulfilled the criteria and have proved you are a suitable candidate you will be issued with a membership card free of charge. You are then able

Pond 1 at Manor House fisheries

to simply turn up and fish. If you are interested in fishing the water or becoming a member please contact the management first.

Cost: Day tickets for adults are £4 for one rod and £5.50 for two rods. After 5pm it is £3. Under-sixteens must be accompanied by an adult and a day ticket for them costs £3 for one rod.

Tickets: Must be purchased in advance from the self-pay box at the entrance to the fishery.

Rules: Fishing is permitted between 7.30am and dusk, with 10pm being the latest you can stay on the waters. No keepnets or groundbait and barbless hooks only. You must dip your landing nets before commencing fishing.

Close season: Open all year.

Disabled Access: Poor.

Matches: Some matches are held for the members but at least one of the ponds will always be available for pleasure anglers.

Car Parking: There is parking at the top of Pond 1 and some parking for Ponds 2 and 3.

Toilets: Yes.

Other Facilities: None.

Nearby Amenities: Copthorne Fisheries can be found only a short distance away. Plenty of pubs and shops on the nearby A6 including The Flag pub and the Lunch Box sandwich bar.

Directions: To find the ponds turn off the A6 at The Flag pub following the signs for Nateby. Soon after passing the post office and primary school on your right-hand side you will see a fish-shaped sign with an arrow on it. Follow this arrow by turning down Hoole Lane and then follow the road round until you enter the farm at the end.

Contact: For further information telephone 01995 602203.

MERE BROW LEISURE LAKES
Off A565, Southport New Road.

Leisure Lakes provides something for everyone as the fishing is complemented (if that is the right word) by a golf driving range, equestrian centre, windsurfing, canoeing, jet skis, mountain biking, quad bikes, a caravan site and car boot sales!

The complex gets very busy in summer and out of the two lakes on site only the right-hand lake can be fished. There are 25 pegs which are located at the top end of the lake. You can drive your car up to the pegs which means you are spared the hassle of carrying your gear a long distance.

Due to the watersports on the lake, the depth is a constant 4ft, but beware you could end up with a windsurfer in your swim. Despite the fact that the complex can get very busy the quality of fishing is very good. There are carp to over 20lb, pike, bream, roach, rudd and tench. There are some good shoals of skimmers which if located and held in your swim can provide an enjoyable day's fishing. The lake is open from 8am in the morning and shuts at dusk.

Cost: £3.20 per rod for adults and £2.20 per rod for OAP and juniors.

Tickets: Day tickets must be purchased on entry to the complex from the kiosk.

Rules: No night fishing.

Close season: Open all year.

Disabled Access: Good. Disabled anglers can drive to several swims.

Matches: Matches can be booked on the lake and are mainly at weekends.

Car Parking: There is a car park on site and you can also park behind the swims.

Toilets: Yes.

Other Facilities: There is a shop and there was a pub on site but this is currently closed. It may be re-opened or converted into a sandwich shop. Do not forget all the other things mentioned in the write-up above!

Nearby Amenities: If you like your fishing more serious or the complex is busy you could try Bannister House Farm just down the road.

Directions: The complex can be found on the A565 to Southport and is well signposted.

Contact: For further details telephone 01772 813446.

MICHELIN LODGE
Netherwood Road, Burnley.

This small idyllic lodge has 10 pegs but there is room for a couple more anglers who can squeeze into undesignated swims. There are carp into double figures, bream and tench to 6lb, roach, perch and gudgeon.

Cost: Day tickets are £2. Membership can be acquired for the Michelin Fishing Club but this is difficult, as you require a sponsor who is a current member of the club or an employee.

Tickets: Must be bought before you fish from the Michelin factory security lodge. The factory is found further along the A6114 if you do not turn right down Netherwood Road.

Rules: No groundbaiting, no boilies.

Disabled Access: Poor.

Car Parking: Small lay-by alongside the water.

Toilets: None.

Other Facilities: None.

Nearby Amenities: Centre of Burnley. Mack's Tackle, 33a Parliament Street, Burnley. BB11 3JU. Tel: 01282 427386. Open Mon-Wed 9am-5.30pm, Thurs 9.30am-6pm, Fri 9am-6pm, Sat 9am-5pm. Rowley Lake is only a few minutes away.

Directions: Following the A6114 out of Burnley town centre from the football ground, take your second right after the traffic lights at Ormerod Road down Netherwood Road. Follow this bumpy road round the back of the factories and the lodge is on your left alongside a small lay-by.

MYRE FOLD FISHERIES
Off the A59 at Clayton Le Dale

There are two waters at this fishery, the willow pond and the lily pond. The willow pond is the larger of the two and it caters for 20 anglers.

It can be found closest to the car park and has an island and depths up to 8ft. The average depth is around 6ft. The willow pond holds carp to 20lb with the average size of fish around the 12lb mark. There are also tench, bream, chub, perch and lots of roach and rudd.

The lily pond has room for only a few fishermen, as it is packed full of lilies, hence its name. The lilies are being cut back and the pond improved and so many more anglers will be able to fish it at the same time. There is an island in the pond and it is slightly shallower than the neighbouring willow pond. The lilies provide protection for carp to 30lb, tench, bream, barbel, chub, perch, roach and rudd.

Cost: Day tickets are £4 for one rod, £5 for two for adults and £2 for OAP, children and disabled.

Tickets: Pay on the bank.

Rules: No groundbait. Fish over 2lb must not be kept in keepnets. Barbless or microbarbed hooks only.

Close season: Open all year.

Disabled Access: Good. You can drive right up to the lily pond.

Matches: Some club matches are held on the willow pond.

Car Parking: Yes.

Toilets: Yes.

Other Facilities: The owner is awaiting approval for a 5 CL touring caravan pitch.

Nearby Amenities: The Royal Oak and Bay Horse pubs and an Indian restaurant on the A59. There is a garage selling chocolate and snacks. There is also a KFC and a Little Chef on the A59 into Preston. Samlesbury Hall. Blue Slate, Knight Bottom Lake, Pine Lodge and Red Rocks Fishery are near. Roe Lee Tackle Box, 336 Whalley New Road, Blackburn. Tel: 01254 676977. Open Mon-Sat 9am-5.30pm.

Directions: From junction 31 of the M6 at Preston follow the A59 towards Clitheroe. After passing Mellor and the Bay Horse pub look out for the Royal Oak pub on your left. When you reach the Royal Oak turn left immediately after the pub and go through the car park. This road takes you down to the fishery which is a couple of hundred yards on your right. You enter the fishery through the gates.

Contact: For more information contact Stanley Alderson on 01254 813437.

OLD HOUSE FARM FISHERY

German Lane, Charnock Richard.

This lake is approximately 5ft deep with a maximum depth of 10ft around one side of the island. There are around 30 pegs on the water. It holds plenty of carp up to 12lb in weight including mirrors, golden and ghost carp. There are also crucians, tench, golden tench, roach, rudd and perch. There are some bream with plans to introduce more.

Cost: £3 a day for adults and £1.50 for OAP and children.

Tickets: Pay at Old House Farm which is across from the lake before commencing fishing.

Rules: No night fishing or boilies. Use of groundbait in moderation only.

Close season: Open all year.

Disabled Access: Good. Although the ground may be uneven in some places.

Matches: A few matches are held on the water.

Car Parking: There is a small car park at one end of the water.

Toilets: None. If you are desperate there may be use of a toilet in the farm yard.

Other Facilities: None.

Nearby Amenities: There are shops and pubs in nearby Euxton. Camelot and Bygone Times can also be found in the area. Lancaster House Farm Fishery is just further up the road. Tackle and bait can be acquired from Don's Tackle, 8 Mill Street, Coppull. Tel: 01257 794040. Open Mon-Sat 8am-6pm, Sun 8am-1pm.

Directions: Take the A49, Wigan Road, past Leyland and through Euxton. After going down the hill you will see a sign for Charnock Richard. After this sign as you start to climb the hill, turn left down German Lane. The fishery and car park are a short distance down here on your right.

Contact: For further information contact Gerry Prescott on 01257 265892.

ORRELL WATER PARK
Lodge Lane, Orrell.

The Orrell Water Park is made up of two lakes. The pleasure lake, which is the Northern Lower Lake is about 6ft deep and has 45 pegs. The Top Lake is normally used as the match lake and it has at least 36 pegs. It has depths between 4ft and 8ft.

The lakes hold a similar mix of fish with carp to 17lb with the average size in the 7lb-10lb bracket, tench to 4lb plus with an average of 2lb, bream, roach, perch, crucian, gudgeon and a few rudd.

The lakes are rotated and so the match lake is open to day ticket anglers for a few months each year to give the pleasure lake a rest and vice versa.

Cost: Day tickets are £3.60 for adults, £2.80 for OAP, disabled, unemployed and students and £2.40 for juniors. Evening tickets, which start after 6pm, are available in June, July and August and cost £2.30, £1.60 and £1.30 respectively. Season tickets are also available priced £72 for adults, £50 for concessions as above and £45 for juniors.

Tickets: All tickets are available on the bank as the water is regularly bailiffed.

Rules: There are no pike present in the lakes and anybody caught spinning or using wire traces will be banned. Other rules include no night fishing, peanuts or associated beans, bloodworm or joker. No keepnets except for in matches. You are also reminded to take all litter home with you or to put it in the nearest bin.

Close season: Open all year.

Disabled Access: Access for the disabled is very good. Orange badge holders can obtain a key to the gate so that they can drive down to the water. There are also disabled platforms to fish from.

Matches: Held on every Saturday and Wednesday in winter. Clubs may also book the match lake to hold their own matches.

Car Parking: Yes.

Toilets: Yes.

Other Facilities: None. On site bailiffs might prove useful in advising on best areas and tactics.

Nearby Amenities: There is a fishing shop opposite the water. Lakeview Tackle, 38 Lodge Road, Orrell. Tel: 01695 625634. Open Mon-Fri 8am-7pm, Wed 9-12.30pm and 3.30pm-7pm, Sat 8am-5pm, Sun 8am-2pm. There are also shops which sell hot pies and food, a chippy and some pubs.

Directions: To find the park leave the M6 at junction 26 and follow the signs to Wigan. When you reach a set of traffic lights turn left to Orrell and then about a quarter of a mile down the road you will reach the traffic lights at The Stag pub, turn left and then left again at the post office onto Church Street. You then need to take a right down Lodge Lane after Orrell railway station, but beware of the dangerous fork in the road and proceed with caution. The car park for the water is on your left-hand side on the opposite side to the Orrell Rugby Union stadium.

Contact: For further information telephone 01695 625338.

PARK QUARRY

Colne.

This quarry has only room for 6 anglers and is run by the Pendle and District Anglers Association. It can only be fished by members of the club and provides some good sport for roach. There are also some perch, pike and the odd carp present.

Cost: Season tickets are £12 for one rod with an extra rod costing an additional £8.

Tickets: Season tickets can be purchased from Mack's Tackle, 33a Parliament Street, Burnley. BB11 3JU. Tel: 01282 427386. Open Mon-Wed 9am-5.30pm, Thurs 9.30am-6pm, Fri 9am-6pm, Sat 9am-5pm. Hyndburn Angling Centre, 71 Abbey Street, Accrington. Tel: 01254 397612. Open Mon-Tues 9am-5pm, Wed 9am-12pm, Thurs 9am-5pm, Fri-Sat 9am-5.15pm.

Rules: Contained on the club card.

Close season: Open all year.

Disabled Access: Poor.

Matches: None.

Car Parking: On Colne Golf Club car park.

Toilets: None.

Other Facilities: None.

Nearby Amenities: The centre of Colne. Foulridge (Lower) Reservoir, Ballgrove Lake and Knotts Lane ponds are all nearby.

Directions: The quarry can be found alongside Colne Golf Club.

PENNY LODGE
Commercial Street, Love Clough.

The lodge holds carp to 12lb, chub to 3lb, tench and perch to 2lb, roach and crucians to a 1lb, bream and golden orfe.

It consists of 15 pegs and has depths from 6ft to 10ft. There are some lilies in the lodge and once they have developed they will provide good cover for the fish and an ideal feature to fish to.

Cost: Day tickets are £4 for adults and £2 for juniors who are 12 and under.

Tickets: Available on the bank.

Rules: No keepnets. Barbless hooks only. No groundbait. No boilies or nuts. No bloodworm or joker. No night fishing.

Close season: Open all year.

Disabled Access: Poor.

Matches: Yes. The lodge can be booked for club matches and the owner intends to run open matches. Information of forthcoming matches can be obtained from the noticeboard at the water.

Car Parking: You can park in the field near the lodge.

Toilets: None.

Other Facilities: None.

Nearby Amenities: Love Clough Angling Club's water is just up the road! Clowbridge reservoir is a mile back towards Burnley on the A682. The Glory pub on the corner of Commercial Street and the A682 sells food. There is a shop half a mile down the road if you turn right out of Commercial Street that sells hot food and snacks. The nearest tackle shop is Mack's Tackle, 33a Parliament Street, Burnley. BB11 3JU. Tel: 01282 427386. Open Mon-Wed 9am-5.30pm, Thurs 9.30am-6pm, Fri 9am-6pm, Sat 9am-5pm.

Directions: To find the lodge take the A682, Burnley Road, through Love Clough and turn down Commercial Street. Follow the road down to the bottom passing the Love Clough Angling Club's waters and the Love Clough Fly Fishery on your right. The lodge is signposted and can be found on your left.

Contact: For further information contact Dave Spivey on 01706 213754.

PERRITES

St. Gregory's Place, Chorley.

This is a rectangular shaped water very close to the centre of Chorley. It is a Withnell Anglers' water and is a popular choice with their members and is one of their main match venues.

There are 30 pegs on the venue which holds carp, tench, bream, roach, gudgeon and the odd perch and chub.

The water is protected by a locked gate and fence and so you must obtain a key once you have gained membership to the club in order to be able to fish it.

Cost: Season tickets for Withnell Anglers are £35 for those who live within the parish of Withnell, which includes Abbey Village, Brinscall and Withnell Fold. Those who live outside the parish boundary can join as associate members for £45.

Tickets: To join the club you must apply to the Membership Secretary at PO Box 41, Chorley, PR6 8JZ. For further information contact Membership Secretary Bernard Wren on 01254 830935.

Rules: Club members only, no day tickets. Maximum of two rods. No night fishing. No keepnets in close season. ALL anglers are responsible for ANY litter found within 10ft of their fishing position.

Close season: Open all year.

Disabled Access: Average.

Matches: Club matches only.

Car Parking: None. You can park your car at the top of St. Gregory's Place.

Toilets: None.

Other Facilities: None.

Nearby Amenities: Chorley town centre. Birkacre Lodges. Tackle and bait can be acquired from Don's Tackle, 8 Mill Street, Coppull. Tel: 01257 794040. Open Mon-Sat 8am-6pm, Sun 8am-1pm.

Directions: From the centre of Chorley take the B5251 down Pall Mall. When you reach a set of traffic lights turn left down Weldbank Lane, then right onto Eaves Green Road and left onto St. Gregory's Place.

PINE LODGE FISHERY

A59, near Clitheroe.

There is a whole array of coarse species stocked in the two lakes at this fishery which is overlooked by Pendle Hill. The main lake, which is directly in front of the car park, is over 8 acres in size and has 120 pegs. Found in its depths, which reach 18ft with an average of 5ft, are carp to 22lb, catfish to 26lb, bream to 9lb and tench to 6lb. The carp average into double figures. There are golden tench, golden rudd, golden orfe, barbel, chub and gudgeon. The perch go to over 4lb and there are loads of roach, rudd and skimmers. The main lake also holds grass carp to 16lb. And if that isn't enough, there are a few trout left over from when the lakes were a trout fishery!

The other lake holds a similar stock. There is the same mix of fish as the main lake but not as many specimens. There are only about 25 pegs and the depths are much shallower with the maximum being around 6ft. The lake is absolutely stuffed with bream and in the future it may become the match lake. There are one or two brown trout in this lake which have sneaked in from the river.

Cost: Weekdays cost £5 for adults and £4 for juniors, OAP and disabled. Weekends are £6 for adults with juniors, OAP and disabled still £4.

Tickets: You can pay at the fishing hut or on the bank. There is an on site bailiff who is there at all times and will collect your money.

Rules: No boilies, bloodworm or joker. Crumb groundbait only. Barbless hooks only. No fish over 1lb to be retained in keepnets. All nets must be dipped before commencing fishing. Net dips can be found at either end of the car park. Night fishing on Friday and Saturdays only.

Close season: Open all year.

Disabled Access: Good.

Matches: Club matches are held on the water and the management also run some matches throughout the summer. There is always room for pleasure anglers when matches are on as they rarely take up more than one bank.

Car Parking: Yes.

Toilets: Yes.

Other Facilities: None. There may be some expansion of facilities in the near future.

Nearby Amenities: Ken Varey's Outdoor World, 4 New Market Street, Clitheroe. Tel: 01200 423267. Open Mon-Sat 9am-5.30pm. The village of

Whalley is a mile away. It has shops, pubs and accommodation. Clitheroe is a couple of miles away and provides similar facilities.

Directions: It can be found directly off the A59 on the right-hand side just before you reach Clitheroe. Take a right at the roundabout outside the fishery entrance.

Contact: For further information contact Richard Harris on 01254 822208.

PLATTS LANE LAKE

Platts Lane, Burscough.

This lake run by the Burscough and District Angling Club, is predominantly a bream water with the species making up a significant amount of the fish in most catches.

With bream to 4lb this makes the water a good club match venue and there are also carp to double figures, tench to 3lb plus, crucians to 2lb, roach, rudd and perch.

The lake can be fished by members of the club or on a day ticket.

Cost: Day tickets are £2.20 for adults and £1.10 for juniors. Membership to the club is £24 for adults and £10.50 for juniors, female adults and OAP.

Tickets: Day tickets are available from the post office on Square Lane. To become a member of the club write to the Membership Secretary at 80 Manor Avenue, Burscough, Lancashire. There is a waiting list in operation for entrance to the adult section of the club.

Rules: No boilies. No bloodworm, joker or associated feed. Day tickets may fish until dusk only. Before 31st May members can fish until 11pm and after 31st May until 31st October members can fish until midnight.

Close season: There is a dual close season in operation. The lake is closed to members between the 15th March and 30th April inclusive and it is closed for day tickets between 15th March and 15th June inclusive.

Disabled Access: Good. The disabled access is via Platts Lane.

Matches: Club matches and visiting club matches are held on the water.

Car Parking: There is a car park located at the end of Platts Lane.

Toilets: None.

Other Facilities: None.

Nearby Amenities: The post office on Square Lane sells crisps, chocolate etc. Bargain Booze (no the club is not encouraging you to drink!) found on the A59 sells hot pies and other snacks. Ray Wright can provide advice, tackle and bait at Burscough Angling Supplies, Lords Gate Lane, Burscough. 01704 896252. Open Mon-Sat 9am -5.30pm. Lathom Fisheries, Hurlston Hall and White Rails Farm are other waters in the area.

Directions: The lake can be found by taking the A59 through Burscough towards Ormskirk. Square Lane is on the left-hand side a short distance after you have passed through the centre of Burscough. Off Square Lane is Chapel Lane which provides access to the water. However, Platts Lane is the main access point and this is further up the A59 on your left after Square Lane.

PREESALL PITS

Acres Lane, Preesall.

These waters are very, very deep as they are former brine pits. There are three pits found on this complex. Two are controlled by the Preesall and District Angling Club and the third is run by the Alkali Angling Club. Both clubs do not issue day tickets.

The Alkali water has 36 pegs and goes to over 40ft deep. You can easily find 20ft of water at the end of your pole. The Alkali water is the first one on your left as you approach the pits. The club keeps specimen records so it is easy to identify the top weights for fish. There are carp to 26lb, tench to 7lb 3oz, bream to 6lb 7oz, eels to 4lb, crucians to 2lb 12oz, rudd to 2lb 3oz, roach to 1lb 13oz and perch to 1lb 10oz.

The Alkali water also holds a lone catfish which weighs around 14lb. The carp average into upper double figures and the tench around 4lb. There are also pike with the fish averaging around 7lb.

The pits controlled by the Preesall Angling Club are even deeper than the Alkali water. The pits go to around 70ft deep! The first pit has 30 pegs and the second 36. They have the same mix of fish as the Alkali pit with carp to 20lb plus, tench to 7lb plus, bream, roach and pike.

Cost: Alkali – Membership to the club costs £24 for the joining fee and £15 a year.

Preesall – Membership to the club is £15 in your first year and £10 for every subsequent year.

Tickets: Alkali – Write to the Membership Secretary at 56 Winchcombe Road, Blackpool. FY5 3HJ. There is a waiting list in operation.

Preesall – Write to the Membership Secretary at 26 Addison Road, Fleetwood. FY7 6UH. Please include a passport sized photograph.

Rules: Alkali – No night fishing. Fishing until 11pm in summer. After September fishing is dawn until dusk. Respect the farmer's land. Full set of rules on club card.

Preesall – There is a long list of rules. A full set is contained in the club card. Maximum of two rods. No unattended rods. No night fishing. No camping. From 1st May until 31st August fishing is allowed between 4am and 11pm. No juniors under 15 unless accompanied by a club member. All carp to be returned to the water immediately. No radios. Dogs to be kept on leads.

Close season: Alkali – Open all year.

Preesall – There is a close season between 1st March and 30th April inclusive.

Disabled Access: Alkali – Poor.

Preesall – There is good access on the second pit as there is a disabled peg.

Matches: Alkali – Club matches only.

Preesall – Club matches only.

Car Parking: There is a car park alongside one of the Preesall Angling Club's pits.

Toilets: None.

Other Facilities: None.

Nearby Amenities: There is the Saracens Head pub which serves food at the top of Back Lane. The nearest tackle shop is Noah's Ark, 41 Lower Green, Poulton-le-Fylde. FY6 7EJ. Tel: 01253 885684. Open Mon-Sat 8am-5.30pm.

Directions: The pits can be found off the B5377, Park Lane, in Preesall. You need to turn down Back Lane and then take a right into Acres Lane which takes you through to the car park.

RAKES BROOK RESERVOIR and RODDLESWORTH (LOWER) RESERVOIR
A675, Bolton Road, at Abbey Village.

These inter-connected reservoirs provide some quality pike fishing. The species run to over 30lb with plenty of the predators into double figures.

The reservoirs are controlled by Withnell Anglers and also contain bream and perch to over 2lb and plenty of roach. The pike often patrol close in and will attack hooked fish or keepnets.

Cost: Day tickets are £3 for adults and £1.50 for juniors and OAP. Season tickets for Withnell Anglers are £35 for those who live within the parish of Withnell, which includes Abbey Village, Brinscall and Withnell Fold. Those who live outside the parish boundary can join as associate members for £45.

Tickets: Day tickets must be obtained in advance either from Brinscall Post Office (open from 6am), School Lane, Brinscall; Withnell Post Office; The Hare and Hounds pub (next to the reservoirs), Bolton Road, Abbey Village; Angler's Den, 19 Blackburn Road, Darwen. Tel: 01254 706713. Open Mon-Sat 9.30am-5pm.

To join the club you must apply to the Membership Secretary at PO Box 41, Chorley, PR6 8JZ. For further information contact Membership Secretary Bernard Wren on 01254 830935.

Rules: Maximum of two rods. No keepnets in the close season. No night fishing. ALL anglers are responsible for ANY litter found within 10ft of their fishing position. Loosefeed only, no cereal groundbaits. Fishing from the dam wall only on Roddlesworth.

Close season: Open all year.

Disabled Access: Poor.

Matches: Club matches. The reservoirs have hosted the National Pike Championship qualifying events.

Car Parking: Yes. There is a car park for Withnell Angling Club at the end of the dam wall at the back of the cottage to prevent people parking on the pub car park and roads.

Toilets: None.

Other Facilities: None.

Nearby Amenities: The Hare and Hounds pub. Angler's Den fishing tackle shop – see address above.

Directions: To find the reservoirs leave the M65 at junction 3. Take the A675, Bolton Road, to Abbey Village and the reservoirs can be found on your left as you leave the village.

Peter Fazakerley and Anthony Machin lie in wait for the predatory Pike at Rakes Brook Reservoir

RED ROCKS FISHERY
Potter Lane, Higher Walton.

This really is a superb mixed fishery which is well worth a visit. The fishery has now added a second lake which can only benefit the main lake and the fishery as a whole.

The main lake has 26 pegs with each fishing platform made of a firm base to provide stability for fishing. The lake is a fairly standard 3-4ft and has an island, some rushes and reeds in the margins. There are tench to 6lb, roach to 2lb and carp up to 15lb. There are also rudd, skimmer bream, perch, crucian carp, gudgeon and the odd chub present.

A secondary stocking of crucians was made and this has increased the number of fish in the main lake. The tench have successfully spawned in the last couple of years and so there are plenty of fish around the 1lb mark to add to the stock of tench in the 2lb-4lb bracket.

The second lake has room for approximately a dozen anglers. It is about a half an acre in size and is stocked with roach, rudd, skimmers and crucians. The emphasis is on quantity rather than quality and so should be ideal for beginners or those after some action.

Cost: Day tickets are £5 for one rod with additional rods costing an extra £1 each.

Tickets: Pay on the bank.

Rules: No night fishing. No groundbait, bloodworm or joker or boilies. Barbless hooks. Children under 16 must be accompanied by a responsible adult. No waste line or litter to be left in pegs. No dogs, fires, loud radios or alcohol.

Close season: Open all year.

Disabled Access: Good. There is a gravel track that runs around the lake and there is a specially constructed disabled peg with a timber floor and sides. The disabled peg is found nearest to the car park.

Matches: Matches are held on some Sunday mornings. The whole lake must be booked by the club holding the event and so the lake will be closed to pleasure anglers. There will be a sign displayed at the fishery warning you of the match or a quick phone call to the owner will confirm whether there is a match on or not.

Car Parking: Yes. At entrance to the fishery.

Toilets: Yes. There is a flush toilet on site.

Other Facilities: The fishery is a Caravan Club certified caravan site. The caravans are sited almost right alongside the water which provides an attractive location and is also very convenient, especially if you have a mountain of gear!

Nearby Amenities: The New Hall Tavern pub can be found half a mile down the road if you turn right at the top of Potter Lane. Blue Slate Fishery is also found in the same area. Nearby tackle shops include Ted Carter's, 85-88 Church Street, Preston. Tel: 01772 253476. Open Mon-Sat 9am-5.30pm, closed Thursdays.

Directions: To get to the fishery take the A6, London Road, out of Preston and soon after crossing the River Ribble keep left at the traffic lights onto the A675. You then need to take the next left at the White Bull, where there is a mini-roundabout, onto Church Brow. The fishery is off this road and can be found down Potter Lane which is on the right-hand side soon after you cross the motorway. There is a little stone cross which is a war memorial at the top of Potter Lane and so it is easy to find.

Contact: For further information contact Bill Cooper on 01772 877277.

REDWELL CARP FISHERY
Near Over Kellet.

This fishery is made up of two inter-connected lakes, one large and one small. The lakes provide 50 pegs and the depth is a fairly consistent 4ft. Shallower water can be found at the far end of the large lake and the deepest spot is behind the island on the small lake at the far corner nearest the big lake.

The lakes provide sport for carp, tench, bream, roach, rudd and golden orfe. There are plenty of skimmer bream to be found in the water. The carp go to around 25lb with the average size around the 10lb mark.

Cost: Day tickets are £5 for adults, £4 for under-fifteens, OAP and disabled and £3 for under-tens. Evening tickets are available for £4. A season ticket is available for £70. Membership costs £20 a year and this allows you to fish for £3.50 a day.

Tickets: Pay at the house before commencing fishing.

Rules: No boilies or trout pellets. Barbless hooks only, a minimum line strength of 6lb, no nuts or bloodworm and all nets must be dipped before being used. There is a maximum rod limit of two rods. No night fishing.

Close season: Open all year.

Disabled Access: Good.

Matches: Some club matches are held on the water but there is always room for the pleasure angler.

Car Parking: Yes.

Toilets: Yes.

Other Facilities: There is a caravan site for 18 touring vans with all the necessary electrical hook up points and accessories. The caravan site office may sell sweetcorn, luncheon meat, barbless hooks and other small items of tackle.

Nearby Amenities: There is a village shop at Over Kellet. Carnforth centre is not far. Tackle and bait can be obtained from Gerry's of Morecambe, 5-7 Parliament Street, Morecambe. Tel: 01524 422146. Open Mon-Sat 9am-5pm, Sun 9am-12pm. Morecambe Angling Centre, Grand Garage, Thornton Road, Morecambe. Tel: 01524 832332. Open every day including Bank Holidays (except Christmas Day, Boxing Day and New Years Day) Mon-Sat 9am-5.30pm, Sun 9am-12pm. Morecambe also has Frontierland and the arcades. The Redwell caravan site could be the ideal base from which to visit the Lake District from. Borwick Lake and Swantley Lake are nearby.

Directions: To find the fishery leave the M6 at junction 35, Carnforth, and head for the village of Over Kellet. On reaching the village green continue straight on and you will find the lakes on your right-hand side a few minutes down the road.

Contact: For further details contact 01524 221979.

RIVER RIBBLE

The River Ribble runs through the heart of Lancashire like a main vein and it provides its anglers with some pulsating sport.

The river holds a variety of coarse species with barbel to double figures, chub to 6lb plus, bream, roach, dace, perch, pike, grayling and the odd carp. Despite the small amount of carp present some have reached the 20lb bracket with one angler taking a near 30lb fish.

The chub seem to average around the 4lb mark with a number of smaller fish coming through. There have been authenticated reports of chub to 7lb. The barbel run from about 1lb right up to double figures with the best going over 12lb. The pike are into double figures but they tend to be localised. The small numbers of carp are best located upstream of the Church Deeps and around the Elston area.

Looking at the fishing rights we start at Clitheroe. Here there are two short stretches. The first runs through the public park at Brungerley and the second at Edisford Bridge. The public park stretch is slightly deeper than the Edisford stretch and can be accessed via the path that runs through the park.

The Edisford Bridge stretch runs for about 1000 yards. A good point of access is by taking the B6243 from the centre of Clitheroe and turning left into the caravan park and following the track to the river.

Both stretches provide good chub fishing but it is advisable to avoid the area around Edisford Bridge during the summer due to the caravan site making it busy. There are some disabled platforms which makes the disabled access very good. Residents of the Ribble Valley can obtain season tickets for the stretch. Weekly and day tickets are available to everyone.

Further downstream at Mitton, there is a stretch controlled by the Environment Agency. This area is more suited to the game angler although some coarse fish are present.

The Warrington Anglers Association have control of a stretch approximately a mile and a half long at Hurst Green. Fishing rights are restricted to one bank and access to the river involves a long walk. The stretch is on the Hurst Green side of the river and starts where Starling Brook enters the Ribble. The stretch runs downstream to Haugh Wood and includes the Dinkley Pool.

The Prince Albert AS has stretches of the Ribble at Dinckley and Ribchester. They also control some rights at Osbaldeston and Red Scar Wood. However, gaining access to fish these stretches is difficult as the angling club has a three year waiting list.

The Ribchester and District Fishing Club control five miles of game and coarse fishing. They have a small 200-yard day ticket stretch which is in Ribchester. It is the length that runs alongside Church Street near the County Primary school. It starts where the stream enters the river just upstream of the school and runs downstream for the 200-yards. Despite being only a short stretch it provides some excellent chub and barbel fishing.

The Northern Anglers Association has a stretch for its members at Balderstone which can be reached by turning down the road opposite the Samlesbury Aerodrome. The area is particularly noted for its chub, barbel and salmon fishing. The precise locations of the stretch are included in the members' book.

We then move onto the areas controlled by the Ribble and Wyre Fisheries Association which is a combination of the Preston Centre of Federated Anglers, Wigan and District A.A. and Bolton Centre. They have joint stretches from Alston Wood, near Balderstone, through Elston and Samlesbury to Red Scar Wood and from the Cuerdale Hall area to Ribbleside Farm. These are good areas to find the chub and barbel but can only be fished by anglers who are members of one of the three clubs.

The Preston Centre also control stretches at the Tickled Trout hotel by junction 31 of the M6, the Church Deeps, the Shawes Arms, Winery Lane and a final stretch from the Continental pub by the railway bridge to Liverpool Road.

The Tickled Trout area is a particular favourite of many anglers and when the river is in form, getting a peg in the best areas can be almost impossible. The Church Deeps and the Shawes Arms are other favoured haunts. The Preston Centre lengths can be fished on a day ticket which should be obtained in advance.

There is a small stretch jointly controlled by the Southport & District A.A. and the Fire Brigade. This can be reached by turning alongside the scout hut in Walton Le Dale on Church Brow. This length is strictly members only.

It is difficult to identify the actual fishing stretches, the best places to fish and access points. The best advice I can give is for you to go and check out the areas of river near you or those you fancy fishing and have a look at what's there and how and what the anglers are catching. Otherwise talk to the staff at the recommended tackle shops.

The Preston Centre and Wigan and District A.A. both produce maps of their fishing rights and I strongly recommend that you purchase one of these as they only cost 50p and £1.25 respectively.

Cost: The Clitheroe stretches are £26.80 for an adult, £12.40 OAP and £9.80 for juniors for a season ticket for Ribble Valley residents only. Weekly tickets are £18 adult and £9 OAP and junior. Day tickets are £7.75 for adults and £3.90 OAP and junior.

The Environment Agency stretch at Mitton is £4.

Membership of the Warrington A.A. is £25 for adults with a £20 joining fee in the first year, £10 for ladies and £5 for juniors.

The Prince Albert AS card costs £66 a year.

Phil Douglas with a double-figure barbel from the lower reaches of the Ribble, near to Preston

The Ribchester stretch is £2.50 for a day ticket for coarse fishing and £10 for game fishing. Membership to the Ribchester and District Fishing Club is a £65 joining fee for adults and then £55 per year and a £15 joining fee for juniors and ladies and then £15 per year. There are also concessions for OAP.

The Northern Anglers card is £20 for adults and £7.50 for OAP and juniors.

The Wigan and District A.A. club card costs £16 for adults, £5 for OAP and only £2 for juniors.

The Preston Centre card is £10 for adults and £5 for OAP and junior. Day tickets are £1.50 and 75p respectively.

Tickets: Tickets for the Clitheroe stretches are available from Clitheroe Tourist Information Centre, 12-14 Market Place, Clitheroe. Tel: 01200 425566. Open Mon-Sat 9am-5pm.

Environment Agency day tickets can be obtained from the Old Stonehouse Restaurant, Mitton Road, Mitton, Whalley. Tel: 01254 826544. Open for tickets 9am-12 midday. If you wish to fish in the afternoon/evening then you can pre-book your ticket the day before and arrange to collect it later in the day. The restaurant is open from 5.30pm Mon-Sun and is an Italian specialising in pastas and pizzas.

For any queries regarding day tickets or fishing on the Environment Agency stretch you can contact their fisheries department on 01772 339882.

Applications to join the Warrington A.A. should be sent to PO Box 71, Warrington. WA1 1LR.

A membership application form can be obtained from www.warrington-anglers.org.uk.

There is a three year waiting list for membership to the Prince Albert AS. If you want to join the list write to the Membership Secretary at 37 Sherwood Road, Macclesfield, Cheshire. SK11 7RR. Please include a stamped addressed envelope so that the Membership Secretary can confirm by return of post that you have been added to the list.

The day tickets for the short Ribchester stretch are available from the Spar shop or the White Bull both found in Ribchester. To become a member of the Ribchester and District Fishing Club there is a two year waiting list. You can put your name on the list by writing to the Membership Secretary at 8 Water Street, Ribchester, Lancashire.

Day tickets for the Preston Centre lengths are available from Ted Carter's, 85-88 Church Street, Preston. Tel: 01772 253476. Open Mon-Sat 9am-5.30pm, closed Thursdays.

The Northern Anglers, Wigan and Preston cards are available from most Lancashire tackle shops.

Rules: It is difficult to include all the rules but a summary is as follows;

Northern Anglers – Parking fee may be required, no dogs, juniors must be accompanied by an adult, no bloodworm or joker or associated feed.

Preston Centre – No camping, fires or dogs. No fishing between 11pm and 4am.

Close season: The river is closed 15th March to 15th June inclusive.

Useful Contacts: Ken Varey's Outdoor World, 4 New Market Street, Clitheroe. Tel: 01200 423267. Open Mon-Sat 9am-5.30pm. Ted Carter's – see address above.

RISHTON PAPER MILL
Hermitage Street, Rishton.

This 30-peg water is very popular with the specimen hunters as the carp run to nearly 30lb. There are many carp in the lake with the average size just below double figures.

There are also bream to 6lb, roach and perch in this venue which is around 8ft deep. It is controlled by the Accrington and District Fishing Club.

Cost: Membership to the Accrington and District Fishing Club coarse section is £40 for seniors and £6 for juniors. A night permit which allows you to fish at night with two rods is an extra £30.

Tickets: The club card is available from Leonard's Angling, 5 Whalley Road, Clayton-le-Moors, Accrington. Tel: 01254 231148. Open Mon-Sat 9am-5pm, Sun 8.30am-11.30am. Roe Lee Tackle Box, 336 Whalley New Road, Blackburn. Tel: 01254 676977. Open Mon-Sat 9am-5.30pm. Hyndburn Angling Centre, 71 Abbey Street, Accrington. Tel: 01254 397612. Open Mon-Tues 9am-5pm, Wed 9am-12pm, Thurs 9am-5pm, Fri-Sat 9am-5.15pm.

Rules: One rod during daylight hours. Two rods at night if you have purchased the extended coarse ticket.

Close season: The club operates an alternating close season between the Haggs Reservoir and Rishton Paper Mill. In the 2000 season the reservoir will be closed between 15th March and 15th June inclusive and in 2001 Rishton Paper Mill will be closed during the same period.

Disabled Access: Average.

Matches: Club matches only.

Car Parking: There is a car park alongside the lake.

Toilets: None.

Other Facilities: None.

Nearby Amenities: There are shops in Rishton and three pubs in a row on the main road, notably the Roebuck. The nearest tackle shop is Leonard's

Angling see address above. Nearest fisheries are Rishton Reservoir, Butts Mill and Haggs Reservoir.

Directions: Leave the M65 at junction 7 and head towards Rishton and Clayton-le-Moors. At the first set of traffic lights, opposite the industrial estate, turn left up Hermitage Street towards Rishton. The lake is on your left as you go up the hill into Rishton.

RISHTON RESERVOIR
A678, Blackburn Road, Rishton.

This Hyndburn and Blackburn A.A. reservoir is cut in two by a railway line. Both parts can be fished and they are joined by a big underwater tunnel. The tunnel can be seen when the reservoir is low otherwise you can tell where it is by looking for an orange post with an orange top situated on the railway line.

The little part, which is closest to the road as you approach the reservoir, often suffers from low levels as the reservoir is used as a top up for the Leeds-Liverpool Canal that runs below it. However, when the levels are high the little part could be worth looking at as the fish like visiting the area. The little part holds 12 anglers. The larger part of the reservoir has 60 pegs and goes to 25ft when the reservoir is full.

The reservoir holds good stocks of carp as several fish from the other club waters have been moved into Rishton. The carp go to 20lb. There are pike to 15lb plus with an average size of around 8lb. Perch to 3lb plus, tench, roach and bream make up the rest of the stock. For those who like fishing for eels, a 6lb specimen has been caught from the reservoir.

Cost: The Hyndburn and Blackburn Angling Association club card costs £38 for seniors, £21 for disabled and £13 for juniors and OAP. A guest ticket is available for £5 but this must be pre-arranged with the membership secretary and you must be accompanied by a member. With such a wide choice of waters I advise you to purchase the club card as it appears a worthwhile investment.

Tickets: The club card is available from most East Lancashire tackle shops, see Butts Mill for details.

Rules: Maximum of two rods. If you are fishing with two rods at least one must be on an audible alarm. No livebaiting.

Close season: Open all year.

Disabled Access: Good. There is access through the park off Cut Lane. The disabled peg is unfishable if the water level is down.

Matches: Club matches and Open matches are held on the reservoir.

Car Parking: At the end of Cut Lane.

Toilets: None.

Other Facilities: None.

Nearby Amenities: Butts Mill, Dickens Street and Fern Gore are the closest Hyndburn and Blackburn A.A. waters. Nearby tackle shops include Leonard's Angling, 5 Whalley Road, Clayton-le-Moors, Accrington. Tel: 01254 231148. Open Mon-Sat 9am-5pm, Sun 8.30am-11.30am. Geoff Done's Fishing Tackle Shop, 12 Southworth Street, Blackburn. Tel: 01254 698161. Open Mon-Thurs 9am-5.30pm, Fri 9am-6pm, Sat 9am-5pm.

Directions: Leave the M65 at junction 6 and take the A678 to Rishton. Just as you enter Rishton you will see the reservoirs on the left. The car park is down Cut Lane which is the first road on your left after the entrance to the boat club. Carry on down the lane passing the park until you cross the cattle grid and the parking is down on your left.

RIVINGTON (LOWER) RESERVOIR
Rivington, Chorley.

The reservoir offers some good sport for perch, pike, roach, tench and bream. However, do not be surprised if you catch one of the rogue brown or rainbow trout in the reservoir. Fishing is restricted to certain stretches of the east bank as most of the reservoir is a designated conservation area.

Cost: The reservoir can be fished on a season ticket which costs £20 for adults and £5 for juniors. There are only 50 tickets available each season.

Tickets: Season tickets must be purchased in advance from the Great House Barn Information Centre. Tel: 01204 691594. (See directions below) All anglers must produce their Environment Agency rod licence when purchasing their ticket.

Rules: Fishing is between the areas marked A-B, C-D and E-F with no casting into the conservation areas. Fishing from sunrise to sunset only. No wading or boat fishing. No under-twelves unless accompanied by and adult. No live baiting, spinning, fly fishing or groundbait. You are supplied with a full set of fishing regulations on purchasing your season ticket.

Close season: Yes. The reservoir is closed from 15th March to 15th June inclusive.

Disabled Access: Poor/Average. The best access is by the castle part of the reservoir.

Matches: None.

Car Parking: Yes. There is parking alongside the Great House Barn Information Centre and further round near the school otherwise you must park on the roadside or in lay-bys.

Toilets: Yes. Next to the Great House Barn Information Centre.

Other Facilities: There is a cafe and gift shop at Great House Barn which is next to the information centre.

Nearby Amenities: Crown Tackle and Bait, 4a Chorley New Road, Horwich. Tel: 01204 668223. Open Mon-Fri 9am-6pm, Wed 9am-12.30pm, Sat 9am-5.30pm. Rivington (Upper) Reservoir is just across the road! There are many walks in the area including one up Rivington Pike. This means there are plenty of car parks and viewing points. However, the area can get busy due to this.

Directions: Leave the M61 at junction 6, Chorley and Horwich and take the A6027 towards Horwich. At the roundabout turn left taking the A673 Chorley New Road through Horwich. After the roundabout in the centre of Horwich turn right onto Lever Park Avenue and this will then take you through to Rivington Lane. You will then find Great House Barn Information Centre on your left.

RIVINGTON (UPPER) RESERVOIR

Rivington, Chorley.

There are some real specimens to be found in the Rivington (Upper) Reservoir. The Rivington and District Pike Angling Club control fishing on the reservoir and to protect the standard of the fishery they reserve pike fishing for members only. There are pike to 32lb with many more fish into double figures.

Before you mourn the loss of such quality fishing you should look at what else is available. There are carp between 14lb and 25lb, chub to 6lb plus, perch to over 3lb, roach and bream. The roach are abundant and there are some beautiful specimens to over 2lb which are like jewels to their captors.

The occasional large trout pops up from time to time as the reservoir used to be a trout fishery.

For those anglers who like to fish the larger waters and prefer the greater bank space then the two Rivington reservoirs could be worth looking at. Not only that but the fishing is cheap compared to many other fisheries.

Cost: Day tickets are £2.50 for adults and £1.50 for juniors, OAP and disabled.

Tickets: Tickets must be purchased in advance from Crown Tackle and Bait, 4a Chorley New Road, Horwich. Tel: 01204 668223. Open Mon-Fri 9am-6pm, Wed 9am-12.30pm, Sat 9am-5.30pm. All anglers must produce their Environment Agency rod licence every time they purchase a day ticket. The water is strictly bailiffed by ALL members of the controlling club. There is a long waiting list for membership to the Rivington and District PAC so it is unlikely that membership can be obtained.

Rules: No pike fishing on a day ticket. Therefore, no spinning, lures, live or deadbaiting. No night fishing. No keepnets. No bread baits or feed. No hemp, bloodworm or joker. No barbed hooks.

Close season: The reservoir is closed from 15th March to 15th June inclusive.

Disabled Access: Poor/Average. The best access is opposite the Rivington

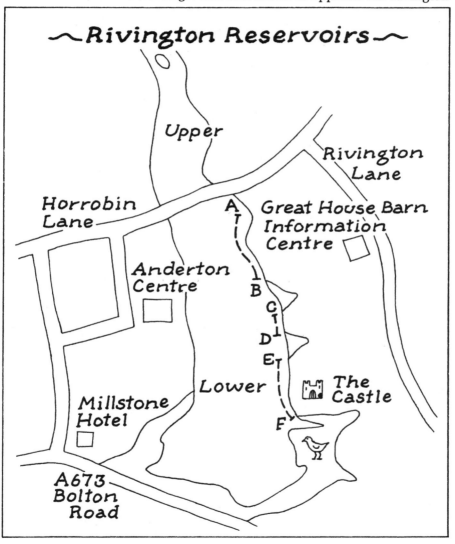

club, where there is a car park. Or, by the Fisherman's Cottage, where you need to go down the 'no through road' right to the bottom where the launch is for the boats.

Matches: None.

Car Parking: Yes.

Toilets: Yes. Next to the Great House Barn Information Centre located above the Lower Reservoir.

Other Facilities: There is a cafe and gift shop at Great House Barn which is next to the Great House Information Centre.

Nearby Amenities: Crown Tackle and Bait see address above. Rivington (Lower) Reservoir is just across the road! There are many walks in the area including one up Rivington Pike. This means there are plenty of car parks and viewing points. However, the area can get busy due to this.

Directions: Leave the M61 at junction 6, Chorley and Horwich and take the A6027 towards Horwich. At the roundabout turn left taking the A673 Chorley New Road through Horwich. After the roundabout in the centre of Horwich turn right onto Lever Park Avenue and this will then take you through to Rivington Lane. If you follow the lane to its end, passing the Great House Barn Information Centre, turn left onto Horrobin Lane and this will then take you between the upper and lower reservoirs. To get to the top end of the reservoir follow Horrobin Lane to the end, turn right onto New Road and then right again onto Nickleton Brow just before crossing the M61. Follow this road past the Yew Tree Inn and if you bear right onto Knowsley Lane this will take you between the upper reservoir and Anglezarke reservoir.

ROACH BRIDGE RESERVOIR

Samlesbury.

This Withnell Angler's reservoir is a good mixed water with plenty of carp, tench, crucian, roach and perch. The roach are particularly abundant and the carp reach double figures.

There are about 20 pegs and the reservoir starts off very shallow before reaching depths of 18ft near the dam wall.

Cost: Season tickets for Withnell Anglers are £35 for those who live within the parish of Withnell, which includes Abbey Village, Brinscall and Withnell Fold. Those who live outside the parish boundary can join as associate members for £45.

Tickets: To join the club you must apply to the Membership Secretary at PO Box 41, Chorley, PR6 8JZ. For further information contact Membership Secretary Bernard Wren on 01254 830935.

Rules: Club members only, no day tickets. Maximum of two rods. No keepnets in the close season. ALL anglers are responsible for ANY litter found within 10ft of their fishing position.

Close season: Open all year.

Disabled Access: Poor.

Matches: Club matches only.

Car Parking: None. Parking is on the verge alongside the red wall.

Toilets: None.

Other Facilities: None.

Nearby Amenities: Samlesbury Hall. Knight Bottom Lake, Blue Slate and Myre Fold fisheries.

Directions: Leave the M6 at junction 31 and take the A59 towards Blackburn. Turn right down Vicarage Lane and continue straight on which takes you into Roach Road. The reservoir is on your left at Roach Bridge. You need to walk into the wood, take the path to the right and upwards which takes you to the dam end.

ROWLEY LAKE
Brunshaw Road, Burnley.

This is quite a large lake found in beautiful surroundings only a few minutes from the centre of Burnley. There are around 40 pegs on the lake which holds carp to over 17lb, tench to 6lb, bream, roach, rudd, perch, gudgeon and a small number of pike which go to nearly 20lb.

The carp average into double figures and the tench average 3lb. Roach up to 2lb in weight have been stocked in the venue.

Cost: Day tickets are £3 for adults and £1.50 for juniors, OAP and disabled. It is one rod per permit. Season tickets are £12 and £7.

Tickets: Day tickets can be purchased on the bank. Season tickets are available from Mack's Tackle, 33a Parliament Street, Burnley. BB11 3JU. Tel: 01282 427386. Open Mon-Wed 9am-5.30pm, Thurs 9.30am-6pm, Fri 9am-6pm, Sat 9am-5pm.

Rules: There are a full set of rules on the day ticket/season ticket but they include night fishing for season ticket holders only which has to be booked through Mack's Tackle.

Close season: Open all year.

Disabled Access: Good. There is a car park very close to the lake and a large disabled platform to fish from at close quarters.

Matches: There are a small number of matches on the lake.

Car Parking: There is plenty of car parking close to the water.

Toilets: None

Other Facilities: Picnic area and play area for the children.

Nearby Amenities: Centre of Burnley. Mack's Tackle – see address above. Michelin Lodge is only a few minutes away.

Directions: From the centre of Burnley follow the signs to Rowley Picnic Site. Passing Burnley Football Club, go up the hill on Brunshaw Street. As the road reaches the top of the hill and sweeps round to the right look for a sign on your left indicating the picnic site. The track is on your left and goes between some houses. There are two gate posts at the entrance which is opposite a bus stop. The track leads to the car parking at the bottom of the hill.

RUFFORD CANAL

This is actually part of the Leeds-Liverpool Canal. The Rufford arm of the canal runs from Tarleton to Burscough where it joins the main canal. It contains roach, skimmers, and a small number of chub and tench. There are also pike and eels present. The fishing on the canal is jointly run by the Preston Centre of Federated Anglers and the Wigan and District A.A.

Cost: It costs £10 senior and £5 junior and OAP to join the Preston and Federated Anglers. They also have stretches of the Leeds-Liverpool Canal, the River Ribble and the River Wyre. The Wigan and District A.A. club card costs £16 for adults, £5 for OAP and only £2 for juniors. The Wigan and District A.A. have several other waters in the Lancashire and Greater Manchester area.

Tickets: The cards for both clubs can be obtained from most tackle shops in the Preston and surrounding area.

Rules: No bloodworm or joker between 1st April and 30th September.

Useful Contacts: Ray Wright can provide advice, tackle and bait at Burscough Angling Supplies, Lords Gate Lane, Burscough. Tel: 01704 896252. Open Mon-Sat 9am -5.30pm. Ted Carter's, 85-88 Church Street, Preston. Tel: 01772 253476. Open Mon-Sat 9am-5.30pm, closed Thursdays.

SHALE HOLES
Railway Road, Brinscall.

Shale Holes is a pond that is split in two by a bed of bulrushes. It has approximately 15 pegs and goes to about 10ft deep.

There are carp, tench, bream, crucians and roach. Despite its size the pond does provide some excellent sport. It is controlled by Withnell Anglers.

Cost: Day tickets are £2.50 for adults and £1.25 for juniors and OAP. Season tickets for Withnell Anglers are £35 for those who live within the parish of Withnell, which includes Abbey Village, Brinscall and Withnell Fold. Those who live outside the parish boundary can join as associate members for £45.

Tickets: Day tickets must be obtained in advance from Brinscall Post Office (open from 6am), School Lane, Brinscall. Day tickets are limited to five per day.

To join the club you must apply to the Membership Secretary at PO Box 41, Chorley, PR6 8JZ. For further information contact Membership Secretary Bernard Wren on 01254 830935

Rules: One rod only for day ticket anglers. Maximum of two rods for club members. No night fishing. ALL anglers are responsible for ANY litter found within 10ft of their fishing position.

Close season: The pond is closed from 15th March until 15th June inclusive.

Disabled Access: Poor.

Matches: Club matches only.

Car Parking: None. You must either park on the roadside at Railway Road, Brinscall or Fellstone View, Withnell.

Toilets: None.

Other Facilities: None.

Nearby Amenities: Croft Lodge is just around the corner. The Cricket Field Lodge, Junior Lodge, Rakes Brook and Roddlesworth are other nearby Withnell Anglers' waters. You are situated almost in the centre of Brinscall so the local shops and pubs are not far away.

Directions: The pond can be approached from two angles. Leave junction 8 of the M61 and take the A674 towards Blackburn and then turn right up Briers Brow which is in front of the Dressers Arms pub. Follow this road until you reach the end and then turn right at the junction onto School Lane. Follow this road to the bottom where it swings sharp left and becomes Railway Road. The pond is through a gate on your left after the cottages. Alternatively, you can access the pond via Bury Road and Fellstone Vale/View, Withnell. There is a path that leads to the pond and it is affectionately known as the 'Yellow Brick Road'.

SHRUGGS WOOD
Off West Paddock, Leyland.

This small lake found near the centre of Leyland was for a long time free fishing. Recently, a group of local anglers have taken over. They have improved the fishery and helped stabilise the state of fishing. The lake has had a chequered past with evidence of illegal stockings (the chub) and rumours of poaching from the water. The club is striving to improve the fishing and are trying to introduce some new marginal plants to help provide spawning areas and protection for the new fry. This will make the lake more pleasant to fish and provide some more features to fish to.

In spring 1999 a stock assessment was carried out by the Environment Agency and it has been rumoured that some of the double figure carp will be removed from the small water to provide more room for the other species.

The lake is only shallow and contains a good head of crucian carp as well as tench, bream, roach, perch, a small number of chub, a couple of catfish and carp into double figures. The price of fishing is still relatively cheap compared to most waters of similar standard.

The lake does get very busy in summer and school holidays due to it being close to several housing estates. It's not the place to fish if you don't like being hemmed in or constantly badgered about whether you've caught anything or not. It can get quite noisy too!

Cost: A season ticket which runs from the 1st January each year costs £10 for adults and £5 for under-sixteens, OAP, unemployed and women. There are also day tickets which cost only £1.

Tickets: Permits are available from Stones Fishing Tackle Shop, 13 Golden Hill Lane, Leyland. Tel: 01772 421953. Open Mon-Tues, Thurs-Fri 9am-5.30pm, Wed 9am-12.30pm, Sat 9am-5pm. Day tickets are available on the bank.

Rules: Night fishing at weekends only. No keepnets between 15th March and 15th June. Landing nets to be used at all times. No groundbait, bloodworm or joker. Loosefeeding only. All fish over 3lb to be returned immediately. Barbless or debarbed hooks up to size 14. Under-tens must be accompanied by an adult.

Close season: Open all year.

Disabled Access: Three disabled platforms.

Matches: Occasional matches are held by the club and are normally on a Saturday. Signs are placed around the water in advance warning that the lake will be shut.

Car Parking: Roadside parking on West Paddock or the nearby Redwood estate is not ideal.

Toilets: None.

Directions: From the centre of Leyland head for the Police Station and Leisure Centre on Lancastergate. After passing the Police Station on your right turn left onto Broadfield Drive and then immediately right onto West Paddock. The lake is on your right behind Worden Medical Centre.

SLATES PITS

Plantation Street, Accrington.

Like Clarendon Street Reservoir, which is just before this fishery, Slates Pits is a Hyndburn and Blackburn A.A. water.

There are four pits which have enough room to accommodate 34 anglers. Pit 1 has 5 pegs and is about 8ft deep. Pit 2 has 6 pegs and is very deep due to slate mining and reaches depths of up to 24ft. Pit 3 has 13 pegs. The three pits have a general mix of coarse fish with carp, bream, tench and roach. Pit 2 holds some roach to over 2lb and is the place to try if you are after a wily specimen. Pit 3 is the one to try if you are after bream as there are some fish to 5lb.

Pit 4 is somewhat of an unknown quantity because despite having 18 pegs it is rarely fished. It does hold roach, perch and gudgeon but really it needs somebody to give it a good go to see what lies beneath its surface, anybody willing to have a try?

Cost: The Hyndburn and Blackburn Angling Association club card costs £38 for seniors, £21 for disabled and £13 for juniors and OAP.

Tickets: The club card is available from most East Lancashire tackle shops, see Butts Mill for details.

Rules: One rod only.

Close season: Open all year.

Disabled Access: Poor.

Matches: Club matches only.

Car Parking: You can park at the end of the road on your left where the bolted gate is. After passing over the cobbled street, the access is to your left.

Toilets: None.

Other Facilities: None.

Nearby Amenities: The pits are close to the centre of Accrington. As well as Clarendon Street Reservoir other Hyndburn and Blackburn A.A. waters in the area include Fern Gore and Kerns Allen. Hyndburn Angling Centre, 71 Abbey Street, Accrington. Tel: 01254 397612. Open Mon-Tues 9am-5pm, Wed 9am-12pm, Thurs 9am-5pm, Fri-Sat 9am-5.15pm.

Directions: The pits can be found off the A680, Eastgate, down Plantation Street in Accrington. At the set of traffic lights on Eastgate turn left onto Plantation Street. The pits are found past the Clarendon Street Reservoir, at the end of Plantation Street down a track.

A right turn at the same set of traffic lights will take you onto Abbey Street where you can find the Hyndburn Angling Centre who will be able to help if you cannot find the pits.

STANLEY PARK LAKE

East Park Drive, Blackpool.

Angling is just one of the many activities offered in Stanley Park. During the peak season the park and lake are packed full of tourists. If you cannot bear a low-speed motor boat churning up your swim every minute or somebody enquiring whether you've caught anything then you should avoid this place like the plague.

Unfortunately, the lake does offer some fantastic fishing and this is why so many anglers put up with the noise and hassle. There are loads of bream to around 4lb which can make up hauls to over 100lb! There are also crucians, tench, carp to double figures including koi, perch, pike and roach.

There are about 30 pegs available on the lake but the angling area, marked off from boaters by wooden posts, makes up only a tiny amount of the area of the lake. This means that the fish can spend the day in safety and move in over the anglers' baits at night. Therefore, the best times are early morning and late evening. At these times the park is also quieter.Early and late season are also better times to fish especially as the lake can suffer from low water levels during the summer. If you want to fish in peace and quiet then winter is your best option but sport can be slow as the fish search out the slightly deeper areas of the lake.

The main tactic seems to be fishing a fairly heavy waggler between the wooden marker posts. If you're fishing the lake for the first time make sure you have some floats capable of being fished three or four rod lengths out. They also need to be able to cope with the swell of a motor boat, you'll soon know what I mean!

Cost: Day tickets cost £4 for adults and £2 for children. Season tickets are available for £10 for adults and £4 for children.

Tickets: Day tickets can be purchased on the bank. Season tickets can be obtained from Anglers World, 183 Preston Old Road, Blackpool. Tel: 01253 764505. Open Mon-Sat 9am-5.30pm.

Rules: One rod per ticket. No night fishing. Day tickets run from when the East gate is opened to 30 minutes before the park is shut. See notices in the park for details. No more than 3lb of groundbait to be used, maximum line strength 3lb, maximum hook size 12, keepnets permitted at the bailiff's discretion, 16th June - 1st October. Keepnets must be emptied at 1pm. No dead or live baiting, no multiple hook rigs and no spinning. No bread baits. Fishing within the marked angling area only.

Close season: Officially, there is a close season although this may no longer be enforced. Please check before fishing.

Disabled Access: Good.

Matches: Some matches may be held on the water.

Car Parking: Yes.

Toilets: Yes.

Other Facilities: Tennis courts, bowling greens, table tennis, croquet, boating lake, gift shop, cafe, trim trail, gardens, athletics track – need I say more?

Nearby Amenities: Anglers World see address above. The centre of Blackpool! (Blackpool Tower, the Pleasure Beach, the Piers, the Illuminations, the traffic and the tourists.)

Directions: Situated in the heart of Blackpool on the A587, East Park Drive, the lake is only a couple of miles from the sea front and Central Pier. It can be found opposite the entrance to Blackpool Zoo and by following the signposts to the Zoo you will come across Stanley Park and its lake.

STANWORTH RESERVOIR
A675, Bolton Road, near Abbey Village.

This reservoir is the second coarse fishing venue controlled by the Blackburn and Nalgo Fishing Club. The reservoir holds 16 anglers and has depths up to 13ft.

It contains carp to 15lb, a small number of bream and tench, roach, rudd, perch, gudgeon and ruffe.

Cost: Membership to the Blackburn and Nalgo Fishing Club for coarse fishing only is a £15 joining fee and £15 per year. The club also controls some trout waters. Full membership costs £110 per season with an initial joining fee of £30.

Tickets: Information and membership details can be obtained from Mr Maddison, 42 Observatory Road, Blackburn. Tel: 01254 53695.

Rules: Barbless hooks preferred. No day ticket anglers unless accompanied by a member and you have pre-arranged your visit.

Close season: Open all year.

Disabled Access: Poor.

Matches: None.

Car Parking: There is parking at the top of the lane and then you have to walk down to the reservoir.

Toilets: None.

Other Facilities: None.

Nearby Amenities: Rakes Brook Reservoir, Withnell Fisheries and the Withnell Angler's waters at Withnell are the closest fisheries. Abbey Village is further up the A675 and there is the Hare and Hounds pub and some shops there.

Directions: The reservoir can be found between Blackburn and Chorley off the A675, Bolton Road, down Stanworth Hall Lane. The reservoir is back under the M65 and between the motorway and the Leeds-Liverpool Canal. The access may be improved, as the club is currently in negotiations.

STOAT HALL FISH PONDS
Back Lane, Croston.

This fishery has matured nicely since I first visited it. If you like to fish small waters that are out in the middle of 'nowhere' then this is a good choice. However, I imagine the fishery itself could get busy as it is only small.

The first pond you come to holds approximately 20 anglers and is full of carp to 12lb. Most of the carp average just under double figures. The pond, which is up to 6ft deep, also holds tench and rudd.

The second pond is much smaller and shallower. It accommodates only six anglers. Despite its size the second pond is a very good bet for quality tench up to 4lb but also holds carp and rudd.

Cost: £3 per rod per day with additional rods costing £1 each.

Tickets: There is a self pay system in operation. If you fail to use it then payment on the bank is double. This fishery has the novel use of a little hatch which you must open to complete your payment. It houses the rules and also pictures of captures from the ponds.

Rules: Fishing is from dawn until dusk only. No keepnets. No breadfeed, bloodworm, jokers or boilies. Loosefeed only and barbless hooks.

Close season: Open all year.

Disabled Access: There is a gate which can be opened to allow access to the ponds.

Matches: None.

Car Parking: There is a small car park at the fishery entrance.

Toilets: A chemical portaloo.

Other Facilities: None.

Nearby Amenities: Croston is a few minutes drive away with its village shops and pubs.

Directions: The ponds can be found down Back Lane, Croston, which is a very narrow road. If you get halfway down the road and think that the fishery cannot be possibly down here then you're probably on the right track! On leaving Croston, pass the railway station and go over the two bridges. You will pass Twin Lakes Trout Fishery and then Back Lane is on your left but it is not signposted. It is opposite the exclusive Bretherton and Croston Angling Club's water.

Contact: For further details telephone 01772 600474.

STOCKY PRIVATE

New Hall Avenue, Blackpool.

This one acre lake is a secret haven only minutes from the hustle and bustle of the centre of Blackpool. In fact, when you're sat on the banks of the lake it is difficult to imagine that you are so close to the tourism, bright lights and busy traffic.

The fishery is a disused clay pit that was first worked in 1892. The pit was first used as a fishery in 1927 and is therefore nicely matured. There are reeds, lilies and overhanging trees in the lake which is on average 5ft. There are some much deeper areas, as you would expect in a lake of this nature.

The fishery has 20 pegs and is described as a 'specimen coarse fishery'. There are carp of all varieties, mirrors, commons, ghost and koi to upper double figures as well as the more sedate crucian carp.

There are quality perch to 4lb plus and tench and bream to over 5lb. There are both silver and bronze bream. There are prize roach to over 3lb. The lake also contains, chub, ide, rudd and golden orfe. There are some big eels to 6lb plus but nobody really fishes for them and who can blame them? The owners have a constant stocking policy and there is a fountain at one end of the lake and this helps aerate the water during hot spells.

Cost: There are no day tickets and membership costs £250 and is limited to 25 people. For people using the caravan site fishing is £10 for 8 hours. The 8 hours can be spread over as many days as you like. Therefore, you can spend four days on the site fishing 2 hours a day for £10.

Tickets: Available from the owners on site. The membership is not yet full and so there is currently no waiting list in operation.

Rules: No keepnets except in matches. Barbless hooks, no boilies, no high protein carp or trout pellets, no hemp and no groundbait. Groundbait is permitted in matches but must be purchased from the owner only – this is so he knows what is going into the water. Three rods maximum. Night fishing Saturday only.

Close season: Open all year.

Disabled Access: Good. There are some disabled platforms easily accessible from the car park.

Matches: The owners holds open matches on the water on Tuesday evenings and Sunday afternoons during the summer. They are open to everyone and to book a place contact the owners. You may pre-book the venue for club matches and the charge is £1 per peg, per hour with a minimum of 10 anglers.

Car Parking: Yes. The car park is locked at night for those who are night fishing.

Toilets: Yes.

Other Facilities: The fishery is a Caravan Club certified location and has room for 5 caravans.

Nearby Amenities: The centre of Blackpool! (Blackpool Tower, the Pleasure Beach, the Piers, the Illuminations, the traffic and the tourists.) Anglers World, 183 Preston Old Road, Blackpool. Tel: 01253 764505. Open Mon-Sat 9am-5.30pm

Directions: Take the M55 to Blackpool. When you reach the end of the motorway you will come to a large roundabout with three sculptures on it. Turn left here down Squires Gate Link Road. Continue on the main road, which becomes Progress Way, and then turn left down Midgeland Road at the first set of traffic lights. Turn left again down New Hall Avenue and follow this track until you come to the entrance to the fishery on your left.

Contact: For more information or to book a caravan or match contact Keith and Pauline Aston-Cardwell on 01253 765498 or 07930 117173.

SUPER STREET

Super Street, Clayton-Le-Moors.

This water holds a good head of roach and skimmers. There are some quality specimens too. There are also some carp present. This water, run by Hyndburn and Blackburn A.A., seems to produce good year round sport. It is only 4ft deep and has 13 swims.

Cost: The Hyndburn and Blackburn Angling Association club card costs £38 for seniors, £21 for disabled and £13 for juniors and OAP.

Tickets: The club card is available from most East Lancashire tackle shops, see Butts Mill for details.

Rules: One rod only.

Close season: Open all year.

Disabled Access: Good.

Matches: Club matches only.

Car Parking: Roadside parking only.

Toilets: None. However, there is a screen to protect you from the overlooking houses!

Other Facilities: None.

Nearby Amenities: Super Street is almost in the centre of Clayton-Le-Moors. There is the Forts Arms and The Royal pub. Leonard's Angling, 5 Whalley Road, Clayton-Le-Moors, Accrington. Tel: 01254 231148. Open Mon-Sat 9am-5pm, Sun 8.30am-11.30am. Rishton Reservoir is the nearest club water.

Directions: Found off the A680, Whalley Road, at Clayton-Le-Moors. It can be best reached via Sparth Road which is directly off the A680.

SWANTLEY LAKE

Near Nether Kellet.

The Lonsdale Angling Club created themselves a superb fishery when they dug the four acre Swantley and stocked it with a wide variety of species.

The lake has matured nicely and the fish have grown considerably since they were first introduced. There are carp to 22lb, tench to 5lb, roach to 1lb, rudd and perch. Bream, chub and crucian carp have also been stocked but they seem to have been the casualties in the competition between the species and are rarely caught.

The lake has about 30 swims and is now for members only after being available to both day ticket anglers and members for many years.

Cost: Membership is £25 per season. Before you become a new member of the Lonsdale Angling Club you must have obtained written permission from the Membership Secretary, Lonsdale A.C., 33 Bridge Road, Greaves, Lancaster. LA1 4UL.

Tickets: Once you have been granted permission to join the club you can purchase your club card from Gerry's of Morecambe, 5-7 Parliament Street, Morecambe. Tel: 01524 422146. Open Mon-Sat 9am-5pm, Sun 9am-12pm. Morecambe Angling Centre, Grand Garage, Thornton Road, Morecambe. Tel: 01524 832332. Open every day including Bank Holidays (except Christmas Day, Boxing Day and New Years Day) Mon-Sat 9am-5.30pm, Sun 9am-12pm. Charlton and Bagnall, 3/5 Damside Street, Lancaster. Tel: 01524 63043. Open Mon-Fri 9am-5.30pm, Sat 9am-5pm, Sun 9.30am-12.30pm. Stephen Fawcett, 7 Great John Street, Lancaster. Tel: 01524 32033. Open Mon-Sat 9am-5pm. Closed Wednesdays.

Rules: A full set of rules is provided in the club card. They include no tiger nuts, peanuts or radio-controlled boats.

Close season: Open all year.

Disabled Access: Poor.

Matches: Club matches only.

Car Parking: There is parking available in the roadside lay-by and at the top of the field.

Toilets: None.

Other Facilities: None.

Nearby Facilities: The village of Over Kellet. Upper Swantley, Redwell Fisheries and Borwick Lake.

Directions: Follow the signposts to Over Kellet from junction 35 of the M6. When you reach the village turn right following the signposts to Nether Kellet passing the Eagle's Head pub on your right. Further along this road are some white railings at a T-junction. Turn left down here and go to the end of this road where you can see the water in front of you just off to the right.

SWIFT'S FARM COARSE FISHERY
Bentley Lane, Mawdesley.

This water run by Lakeside Field Sports has approximately 15 pegs. It contains the usual mix of fish which seems to be common with most fisheries in this area. It has carp to double figures, tench, bream, roach, rudd, and perch.

Cost: £3 per day for adults and £2 for OAP, children. Double, if you are caught on the bank without your ticket.

Tickets: A self pay system is in operation and the pay cabin is alongside the fishery.

Rules: No night fishing, dawn until dusk only. No breadfeed, boilies or keepnets. Barbless hooks only.

Close season: Open all year.

Disabled Access: Poor. If you can get your car onto the field during summer then some pegs may be reached but are still some distance away.

Matches: A few matches are held on the water.

Car Parking: There is a small car park opposite the water in the farm yard. Beware it could get quite tight. Parking is allowed in the field adjacent to the water in summer.

Toilets: None.

Other Facilities: None.

Nearby Amenities: The Brook House pub is just down the road. Eccleston with its shops and pubs is not far. There are also Camelot, Bygone Times, Cedar Farm and Eccles Farm tourist attractions in the area. Charity Farm Fishery is around the corner. Tackle and bait can be acquired from Don's Tackle, 8 Mill Street, Coppull. Tel: 01257 794040. Open Mon-Sat 8am-6pm, Sun 8am-1pm.

Directions: To find the fishery follow the signposts for Camelot and Bygone Times and leave the A49, Preston Road, as instructed. Pass Camelot and when you reach the end of Park Hall Road turn right towards the centre of Eccleston. Soon after passing Bygone Times on the left and Pontins headquarters on the right you need to turn left down Bannister Lane. Follow this road and before you reach the Brook House pub on your left turn right down Bentley Lane. The fishery car park is a short distance down here on the left. The actual water is across the road on your left where the road disappears round the bend. There is a sign and a gate leading you into the correct field.

Contact: For further information contact Clare Fiddler of Lakeside Field Sports on 01257 453777.

THURSLAND HILL FARM

Moss Lane, Thurnham, near Glasson.

Like so many other fisheries that started out with just one pond or lake, Thursland has now extended its number of waters to two.

The original pond holds 17 anglers and despite its small size it is still more popular. When you know the stocking of this pond then you will realise why it is so busy. There are carp to 25lb with the average size being 8lb. There are tench to 6lb with an average of 4lb and roach to over 1lb.

The newer small lake has an island in the middle which allows 33 anglers to fish at once in relative comfort. There is a wider range of species in the lake than the pond and although the sizes are smaller the fish are growing fast.

The lake was opened in 1998 and within a couple of years the carp had reached over 6lb in weight and these are expected to rise rapidly. There are also tench, crucians, roach, rudd and perch.

If the pond is overcrowded then it might be worth trying your luck on the quieter lake although in time I expect the pressure to spread out evenly over the two waters. The depths on the waters vary but on average they are probably 5ft deep.

Cost: Day tickets are normally £4 for one rod and £7 for two for adults and £2.50 a rod for OAP and disabled. However, due to the popularity of the pond in summer, it is £5 for one rod and £8 for two for adults and £3.50 a rod for OAP and disabled. The lake is the same price throughout the year but if the venue becomes busier then this may be reviewed. Spectators are charged 50p each.

Tickets: There is a self pay system in operation which is located on the car park. You will be charged double if caught on the bank without a ticket and spot checks are carried out.

Rules: Day tickets run from 6am-9pm. No groundbait, keepnets or lines below 4lb breaking strain. You must also use barbless hooks. Children under 16 must be accompanied by an adult. Night fishing which runs from 9pm-6am is by prior arrangement only and is strictly limited. The line restriction does not currently apply to the lake but once the fish get bigger this rule will be enforced on both waters.

Close season: Open all year.

Disabled Access: Average. Although there is an separate area for disabled parking by the cattle grid which allows easier access to the water.

Matches: The owners run matches on the lake every Sunday through August and September. There are a few club matches held on the lake also. There are always warning signs displayed in advance.

Car Parking: Yes.

Toilets: Yes.

Other Facilities: Snack bar with ice cream, chocolate, crisps, hot and cold drinks. There are bacon butties and burgers available at weekends.

Nearby Amenities: There are pubs and shops at Cockerham, Glasson Dock and Condor Green which are all a couple of minutes drive away.

Directions: To find the venue turn off the A6 onto Cockerham Road following the signs for Cockerham and Glasson Dock. When you reach the Manor Inn turn right and follow the road through to Thurnham. Once you have reached this village, take your next left down Moss Lane and the lake is signposted down here on the left-hand side.

Contact: For further information telephone 01524 751076.

TOAD HALL FARM
Brock Road, Inskip.

There are three ponds to be found on this fishery. They all average about 8ft-10ft. The first pond holds carp to 14lb, tench and bream to 3lb, roach to 2lb and a few perch to 3lb plus. There is room for 10 anglers on the first pond.

The second pond has room for only 5 anglers and holds carp to 10lb and tench. The third pond has 8 pegs and has the same mix of fish as pond 2.

Cost: £3 per day. Season tickets are available for £30.

Tickets: Pay at the farm before commencing fishing. If it is early morning your money will be collected on the bank later.

Rules: No groundbait, bloodworm or joker. Barbless hooks only. Fish over 2lb not to be retained in keepnets. Fishing from dusk until dawn only.

Close season: Open all year.

Disabled Access: Good. If the field is dry you can park by the ponds otherwise there is a track near the ponds.

Matches: Matches are mainly held during winter.

Car Parking: Yes.

Toilets: None.

Other Facilities: None.

Nearby Amenities: The village of St Michael's. Briarcroft and Wyreside Fisheries, Hudsons Farm.

Directions: To find the fishery turn off the A6 in Bilsborrow following the signs for Myerscough College and Guy's Thatched Hamlet. Carry straight on and follow the signs for Great Eccleston taking care not to turn towards St Michael's. After a sharp left-hand bend you need to turn right down Moss Lane which leads onto Brock Road. The farm is the first one on your left and is signposted.

Contact: For further information contact 01995 679665.

TURBARY HOUSE FISHERY
Chain House Lane, Whitestake.

This lake started out as a trout fishery but it soon proved itself to be a prolific coarse fishery. The fishery was then closed for several years and this allowed the fish to pile on the pounds in relative safety.

Since the venue was re-opened, the biggest carp caught weighed 28lb. There is at least one other carp in the 20lb bracket present. The average fish caught is around the 7lb mark.

The lake is not just a carp water though. It has room for approximately 20 anglers and is full of crucians, bream, tench, roach, rudd and perch. There are plenty of skimmers. The depths vary from 8ft-3ft and there are plenty of features to fish to.

Being located in the grounds of a garden centre you may get disturbed by the customers especially at weekends.

Cost: Day tickets cost £5 for two rods and run from 8am-6pm due to security reasons. Juniors can fish for £3. The lake may be open for a limited number of evenings each year or by prior arrangement.

Tickets: Available on the bank.

Rules: No keepnets except in matches. Groundbait may be restricted/banned in adverse weather conditions – e.g. hot spells when the water level is down. No floating baits. No bloodworm and joker between April and September inclusive. Barbless hooks. No dogs.

Close season: Open all year.

Disabled Access: Average.

Matches: Yes. Club matches can be booked on the water.

Car Parking: Yes.

Toilets: Yes. In the garden centre. Please note the fishery and garden centre are separate businesses.

Other Facilities: Cafe in the garden centre. The cafe sells highly recommended breakfasts which are popular with the anglers!

Nearby Amenities: The Farmers Arms pub is a couple of minutes past the garden centre. Lostock Tackle Box, 16 Watkin Lane, Lostock Hall, Preston. Tel: 01772 626585. Open Mon-Thurs 7.30am-6pm, Fri 7am-8pm, Sat 6am-6pm, Sun and Bank Holidays 7am-12pm. Stones Fishing Tackle Shop, 13 Golden Hill Lane, Leyland. Tel: 01772 421953. Open Mon-Tues, Thurs-Fri 9am-5.30pm, Wed 9am-12.30pm, Sat 9am-5pm.

Directions: Taking the A582 out of Preston town centre follow the bypass towards Leyland until you reach a set of traffic lights. Turn right here onto Chain House Lane and the garden centre is shortly on your right. The actual garden centre has now been renamed Trebaron. Turn into the entrance of

Trebaron garden centre and the access to the fishery is via the nursery at the bottom of the car park. Go down to the potting sheds and turn left.

Contact: For further information contact John on **01772 697337.**

Turbary House Fishery is heavily lined with trees on two sides

TWINE VALLEY

Near Ramsbottom.

This 30-plus-peg lake provides good sport for carp, chub, bream, roach and perch. The lake is approximately 4.5 acres and has depths to 27 feet.

The carp run to around 10lb, the bream and chub average around 2lb and there are some large roach and perch to 2lb.

There is also a trout lake at the fishery, which like the coarse lake, can be fished on a day ticket.

Cost: Day tickets are £6 for adults and £3 for juniors, OAP and disabled. Trout fishing is £10 for 5 hours with a two fish limit.

Tickets: Must be purchased from the Fisherman's Retreat, the on site pub and restaurant, before commencing fishing.

Rules: No groundbait. Barbless hooks only. No night fishing.

Close season: Open all year.

Disabled Access: Average.

Matches: Some club matches are held on the water. There are signs displayed for pleasure anglers warning them of forthcoming matches.

Car Parking: Yes.

Toilets: Yes.

Other Facilities: The Fisherman's Retreat serves pub lunches.

Nearby Amenities: The fishery is close to Ramsbottom. The nearest tackle shop can be found in Bury: Fisherman's Way, 45 Walmsley Road, Bury. Tel: 0161 7611359. Open Mon-Sat 9am-6pm.

Directions: Take the A56 from Bury. After going over the M66 turn right into Bye Road after passing a Post Office on your left. Following the signs for the Fisherman's Retreat, turn right onto Bamford Road and then left down Bury Old Road and then right onto Riding Head Lane.

Contact: For further information contact Hervey Magnall on 01706 825314.

UPPER SWANTLEY

Near Nether Kellet.

This is the third water controlled by the Lonsdale Angling Club. The small water comfortably holds 6 members at once and is especially noted for its stocks of silver fish.

The roach and perch are abundant in the water and the odd tench that make an appearance are normally a welcome break from the silver fish.

Cost: Membership is £25 per season. Before you become a new member of the Lonsdale Angling Club you must have obtained written permission from the Membership Secretary, Lonsdale A.C., 33 Bridge Road, Greaves, Lancaster. LA1 4UL.

Tickets: Once you have been granted permission to join the club you can purchase your club card from Gerry's of Morecambe, 5-7 Parliament Street, Morecambe. Tel: 01524 422146. Open Mon-Sat 9am-5pm, Sun 9am-12pm. Morecambe Angling Centre, Grand Garage, Thornton Road, Morecambe. Tel: 01524 832332. Open every day including Bank Holidays (except Christmas Day, Boxing Day and New Years Day) Mon-Sat 9am-5.30pm, Sun 9am-12pm. Charlton and Bagnall, 3/5 Damside Street, Lancaster. Tel: 01524 63043. Open Mon-Fri 9am-5.30pm, Sat 9am-5pm, Sun 9.30am-12.30pm. Stephen Fawcett, 7 Great John Street, Lancaster. Tel: 01524 32033. Open Mon-Sat 9am-5pm. Closed Wednesdays.

Rules: A full set of rules is provided in the club card. They include no tiger nuts, peanuts or radio-controlled boats.

Close season: Open all year.

Disabled Access: Poor.

Matches: Club matches only.

Car Parking: There is parking available in the roadside lay-by for about 2 or 3 cars.

Toilets: None.

Other Facilities: None.

Nearby Amenities: The village of Over Kellet. Redwell Fisheries and Swantley Lake are the nearest venues.

Directions: Full directions are contained in the club card but the water is not far from Swantley Lake and is just past the gas compressor works and the Tarmac quarry.

VERNON'S LODGE
Factory Lane, Penwortham.

This three acre water is hidden behind Vernon's Mill and access can pose a bit of a problem. The far end is unfishable due to the number of trees surrounding it and it is impossible to walk all the way round with your tackle. This means you must decide which side you want to fish before making your way to the water. One side can be reached by turning right soon after you have entered the grounds of the mill and following the road until it comes to a dead end with a gate to enter the fishery. The far side of the lodge can be reached by going straight through the factory grounds and reaching a car park up on your right at the end of the road. The deepest water is found at the factory end of the lodge.

Species present are bream, tench, roach, eels and carp to around 15lb.

Cost: A season ticket costs £15.

Tickets: Available from Lostock Tackle Box, 16 Watkin Lane, Lostock Hall, Preston. Tel: 01772 626585. Open Mon-Thurs 7.30am-6pm, Fri 7am-8pm, Sat 6am-6pm, Sun and Bank Holidays 7am-12pm. Ted Carter's, 85-88 Church Street, Preston. Tel: 01772 253476. Open Mon-Sat 9am-5.30pm, closed Thursdays.

Rules: No bloodworm or joker, livebaiting or fishing at night. No trout pellets. One rod per licence and no fishing behind the island. Under-twelves must be accompanied by an adult.

Close season: 1st April - 31st May.

Disabled Access: Very Poor.

Matches: The lodge is closed on every Tuesday during summer and some Sundays for matches. The dates are displayed in advance.

Car Parking: At the end of the track there is a car park.

Toilets: None.

Other Facilities: None.

Nearby Amenities: Preston, Penwortham and Lostock Hall. Lostock Tackle Box see address above. Nearest fisheries are Turbary House Fishery and Farington Lodges.

Directions: To find the lodge take the B5254, Leyland Road, through Lower Penwortham and then turn down Factory Lane. The mill is found at the end of this road after you have passed under the railway bridge.

WATERY LANE LODGES
Watery Lane, Darwen.

There are two lodges run by the Newrad Fisheries Club. But before I provide you with the details on the fishery I have got a little brain-teaser for you all. The club has been in existence for over 20 years, but how did it choose its name?

The Top Lodge can be fished by the members of the club and on a day ticket. It has 12 pegs, six of these are disabled platforms. The average depth is about 10ft. It holds tench to 4lb, bream to 3lb, crucians, roach and hybrids.

The Bottom Lodge is for members only and contains a better stamp of fish. There are carp to 27lb with the species averaging well into double figures. There are tench to 7lb, bream to 4lb, roach and crucians. The tench average around 2lb. There are lots of big roach with fish over 2lb caught every season. There are 11 pegs on the Bottom Lodge which has depths ranging between 2ft and 10ft.

Still not solved the riddle? Clue: It is something to do with where the lodges are located.

Cost: Day tickets for the Top Lodge only are £3 and £1.50 for OAP and disabled. Membership to the club is £27.50 in your first year and £22 if you are already a member.

Tickets: Day tickets are available from Angler's Den, 19 Blackburn Road, Darwen. Tel: 01254 706713. Open Mon-Sat 9.30am-5pm.

You can apply to the club for membership by writing to the Membership Secretary at 47 Garden Village, Darwen.

Rules: They are displayed on the noticeboard at the water, on the day ticket and club card. Night fishing for members only. No keepnets for one month around May to June.

Close season: Open all year.

Disabled Access: Excellent. The Top Lodge is particularly noted for its disabled facilities.

Matches: Club matches only.

Car Parking: There is plenty of roadside parking.

Toilets: There are plans in place for a disabled toilet. It is hoped construction will be underway soon.

Other Facilities: None.

Nearby Amenities: There are some shops 200 yards away. The Park Hotel and The Swan pubs are on the main road. Both serve hot snacks/bar meals. Nearest tackle shop is the Angler's Den – see address above. Nearby fisheries include Hoddlesden Reservoir, Rakes Brook and Roddlesworth Reservoirs and Withnell Fisheries.

Directions: Leave the M65 at junction 4. Follow the signs for the A666 and take this road right through the centre of Darwen. Watery Lane is on your left just before you reach the cemetery on your right. The lodges are on your left behind the wall and gates, before you reach the industrial estate.

Answer: Newrad is Darwen spelled backwards!

WALVERDEN RESERVOIR
Brunswick Street, Nelson.

This reservoir is a conservation area and so is shut during the old close season. However, the quality of fishing is not affected by the short break and carp to 24lb, bream, tench, roach and perch can be caught.

Cost: Season tickets are £18.70 for adults (a second rod costs an extra £9.35) and £10 for juniors and OAP (second rod costs £5). Day tickets are £2.80 for adults and £1.50 for juniors and OAP with an additional rod costing £1.40 and 75p respectively.

Tickets: Both day and season tickets can be obtained from the bailiffs on the bank. The season ticket requires a passport sized photograph for your card.

Rules: No boilies or livebaits. Members are allowed to night fish but they must pre-book at the Pendle Leisure Centre in Colne on 01282 661248.

Close season: Closed between 15th March and 15th June inclusive.

Disabled Access: Average. Some pegs on the left-hand side may be reached by the disabled.

Matches: To book a match on the water contact the Pendle Leisure Service on 01282 661230.

Car Parking: Yes.

Toilets: None.

Other Facilities: None.

Nearby Amenities: Nelson town centre. Boyces Fishing Tackle, 44 Manchester Road, Nelson. Tel: 01282 614412. Open Mon-Sat 9am-5pm except Tues 9am-1pm.

Directions: The reservoir can be found on the outskirts of Nelson at the top of Brunswick Street, which is close to the railway station in Nelson.

Contact: For further information contact the Pendle Leisure Service on 01282 661230.

WHITE RAILS FARM
Asmall Lane, Ormskirk

This small fishery is pleasantly surrounded by trees which provides protection for both the angler and the fish.

There are carp to 17lb including commons, mirrors, ghost and koi. The carp average around 10lb. There are also tench to 4lb and perch.

Cost: Day tickets are £3 for two rods.

Tickets: Pay on the bank.

Rules: No groundbait or boilies. No keepnets. No night fishing. No litter! Please place all your rubbish in the litter bins provided.

Close season: The fishery is closed from the 31st October to the 1st April.

Disabled Access: Poor.

Matches: None.

Car Parking: Yes. To the right alongside the large warehouse.

Toilets: None.

Other Facilities: None.

Nearby Amenities: There is a small supermarket if you turn right out of the fishery, next right and then right again. There are plenty of pubs in the vicinity. Ormskirk centre is not far. The nearest tackle shop is Burscough Angling Supplies, Lords Gate Lane, Burscough. Tel: 01704 896252. Open Mon-Sat 9am-5.30pm. Fisheries in the area include Hurlston Hall, Platts Lane and Lathom.

Directions: Take the A59 from Preston to Liverpool. When you reach the main traffic lights in Ormskirk at the junction of the A59 and the A570 continue straight on towards Liverpool. At the next roundabout go right down Cottage Lane. This then leads you onto Asmall Lane. The fishery is on your right immediately after White Rails Mews.

WILLOW BRIDGE FARM FISHERY

Catforth.

This is another small fishery but it is rather unique as it provides some rather unusual sport. The stock is made up of ghost carp, albino grass carp, golden tench, roach and skimmer bream.

The fishery is quite new and so the fish are growing fast. There are 13 pegs on the water with the depth being around 10ft.

There is a second lake which will probably be open from the middle of 2000 onwards. It is much larger than the first lake with around 40 pegs. However, before it can be opened the lake requires some remedial work and access to it, which is across some fields, needs to be opened up.

Cost: Day tickets are £3.

Tickets: Must be purchased from the farm before going down to the fishery. (See directions)

Rules: Barbless hooks only. Dip nets before commencing fishing. No night fishing.

Close season: Open all year.

Disabled Access: Average. The peg nearest the car park is probably the best. Some people may find it difficult getting to the pegs as you have to go down to them. However, this does provide the angler with some protection from the wind and the weather.

Matches: None.

Car Parking: Yes.

Toilets: None.

Other Facilities: There is a caravan site for 5 caravans by the lake with running water and refuse facilities.

Nearby Amenities: The Catforth Gardens, which is just before the fishery, is a well-known Nursery with plenty of gardens to walk round and plants to buy. There is the Bay Horse pub in the centre of Catforth on Bay Horse Lane which serves food. There are some shops in Catforth. The nearest tackle shops are Ted Carter's, 85-88 Church Street, Preston. Tel: 01772 253476. Open Mon-Sat 9am-5.30pm, closed Thursdays. M.S. Jackson, 33 Moor Lane, Preston. Tel: 01772 558670. Open Mon-Tues, Thurs-Fri 9am-5.30pm, Wed 9am-12pm, Sat 8am-6pm, Sun 6.30am-10.30am (Sundays May-September only).

Directions: Leaving the M6 at junction 32 at the Broughton motorway roundabout take the A6 towards Broughton. When you reach the traffic lights at the crossroads turn left down Woodplumpton Lane. Follow the main road and then turn right towards Catforth onto Woodplumpton Road. After crossing the Lancaster Canal, turn left down School Lane following the sign for Catforth Gardens. After passing the school, turn left onto Catforth Road and then right down Benson Lane. The road will take a sharp left and this leads you onto Roots Lane. The Gardens are 100 yards down here on your right, followed by the entrance to the farm on your right and then the last right before the bridge back over the canal is the entrance to the fishery.

Contact: For further information contact Bill Moore on 01772 690269 (after 7pm) or 07712 804921.

WITHNELL FISHERIES
Oakmere Avenue, Withnell Fold.

Consisting of three reservoirs, all between three and four acres, the fisheries provide plenty of good swims and quality fishing for the members of the Withnell Fisheries Angling Club.

The Top Reservoir on Oakmere Avenue has 30 pegs and is up to 22ft deep. The Bottom Reservoir has 40 pegs and has roughly the same depth. The third reservoir found across the main road in the village is known as Sans and has depths up to 12ft.

The reservoirs hold the same mix of fish with carp to double figures, tench to 11lb plus, bream to 7lb and roach. The are some good shoals of bream which average between 3lb-4lb and the tench average around the same mark. The roach are of a high average size with some beautiful specimens around three quarters of a pound.

Cost: Season tickets currently cost £55.

Tickets: There is a waiting list in operation. Information is available from the Company Secretary at 279 Hulton Lane, Bolton. BL3 4LF.

Rules: No members under the age of 18. One rod only until 1st October when two rods are permitted until the season ends. A passport-type photograph must be supplied for your season ticket. A full set of rules will be provided once you have gained membership to the club.

Close season: There is a close season in operation on the water.

Disabled Access: Average. Access on Top Reservoir only.

Matches: Club matches only.

Car Parking: There is room for several cars at the top of Oakmere Avenue.

Toilets: None.

Other Facilities: None.

Nearby Amenities: Cricket Field and Junior Lodge are very close. Rakes Brook and Roddlesworth and Heapey are also in the same area.

Directions: Leave the M65 at junction 3 and at the roundabout take the A674 towards Higher Wheelton. You will soon reach the small village of Withnell Fold. If you turn left onto Oakmere Avenue and go straight up the track it will reveal two reservoirs. If you turn right almost opposite Oakmere Avenue and go into the main part of Withnell Fold the third water can be found close to the mill at the bottom.

WOODFOLD FARM FISHERIES

Near Beacon Fell Country Park.

The fishery is made up of five lakes with each lake being individually named and providing a slightly different variety of species and weights. However, the owner is concerned about the standard of his fishery and so only serious anglers who show concern for the countryside are encouraged. Therefore, I cannot recommend the fishery to those who are inexperienced anglers or have inadequate tackle.

The fishery does provide some good sport. Woodfold Waters contains roach, tench, crucian carp, perch, commons and mirrors to 12lb. There are 23 pegs with depths ranging from 4ft-8ft.

Fylde View has a similar selection of species to Woodfold Waters with tench being the speciality for this lake with specimens over 7lb on offer. There are several good tench caught every year. Fylde View has depths up to 12ft and has 30 pegs.

If you are after quality roach, rudd and perch then Beacon Water is the lake to choose. All three species can be caught over the magical two pound and the lake also offers some carp, skimmer bream and crucians. The Beacon Water has 23 pegs with depths from 5ft-12ft.

Cornthwaite Lake and Whippercroft both offer rudd, bream and chub and they are the lakes which provide the best sport for bream. The original bream stock ranged from 2lb to 7lb and after successful spawning a number of skimmer bream can now be caught. Both Cornthwaite and Whippercroft have 12 pegs with depths to 8ft. There are plans for a sixth lake.

Cost: Season tickets are £95 a year. Day tickets are currently available priced £7. From April 2000 the fishery may be available on season ticket only to protect the quality of the fishery.

Tickets: Pay on the bank for day tickets.

Rules: The owner enforces the rules and anybody caught breaking them or misbehaving will be strictly dealt with. No boilies, bloodworm or groundbait. Barbless hooks only. No tiger nuts. Fishing from dawn until dusk only.

Close season: Open all year.

Disabled Access: Poor.

Matches: None.

Car Parking: Yes.

Toilets: Yes.

Other Facilities: None.

Nearby Amenities: Wyreside, Lyndhurst and Horns Dam are the nearest fisheries. Beacon Fell Country Park.

Directions: Leave the A6 between Bilsborrow and Catterall and turn onto New Lane, which is alongside a petrol station, following the signs for Beacon Fell Country Park. In the centre of Inglewhite, turn left at the village green; go to the end of this road and then turn right towards Chipping and Bleasdale. Finally turn right again following the sign to Woodfold Fisheries. Once you have located the road down to the fishery turn right when you enter the farm yard and it will take you to the car park situated round the back of the farm.

Contact: For more information telephone John Cornthwaite on 01995 640347.

WORTHINGTON LAKES

A5106, near Standish.

The majority of this complex is now actually in the county of Greater Manchester and not Lancashire. Only the most northern tip of the top reservoir, Adlington No 3, is located in the Red Rose county. The lakes are made up of three reservoirs, the first being Worthington No 1, followed by Arley No 2 and finally as I have already mentioned Adlington No 3.

Worthington holds some very good roach and perch with specimens over 2lb being caught. One lucky angler made a catch of four bream for 34lb with the biggest weighing 10lb. However, there appears to be only be a small number of bream in Worthington and that may account for their size. There are also some barbel up to 9lb.

Arley contains a bigger variety of species with roach, bream, perch and a number of carp well into double figures.

Adlington provides good sport for roach, rudd, perch and the odd carp.

Cost: The superb Wigan and District A.A. club card costs £16 for adults, £5 for OAP and only £2 for juniors. Day tickets are £2, £1 and 30p respectively.

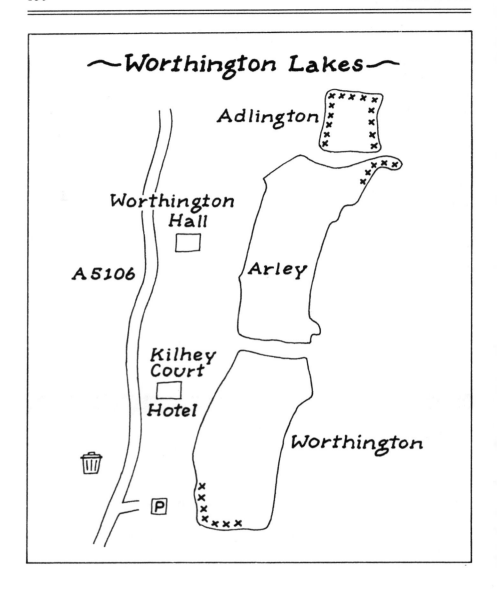

Tickets: Day tickets are available on the bank from the patrolling bailiffs. The club card is available from most tackle shops in Lancashire.

Rules: There are quite a few rules for Worthington Lakes and these include loose feeding only with maggots, casters and worms, the use of cereal baits is strictly prohibited. No bread, hempseed, boilies, sweetcorn, maple peas, chick peas, black-eyed beans, peanuts, tiger nuts etc. may be used. Spinning, flyfishing, live or deadbaiting is strictly forbidden. No night fishing. Adults are restricted to two rods and juniors one rod.

Close season: Arley and Adlington are shut during the close season but Worthington is open for trout fishing. See club card for more details.

Disabled Access: Poor.

Matches: A few club matches are held on Arley.

Car Parking: Car park at one end of the lakes. Anglers also have permission to park on the Kilhey Court Hotel car park but *please* use the area of car park furthest from the entrance to the Hotel.

Toilets: Yes.

Other Facilities: None.

Nearby Amenities: Standish is only a few minutes away. Dream Angling Tackle and Bait, 63 Preston Road, Standish. Tel: 01257 472707. Open Mon-Sat 9am-5.30pm.

Directions: The complex can be found close to the centre of Standish. If you take the A49 towards Wigan when you reach Standish take the B5239. This takes you down Rectory Lane and at the end of this road turn left and the lakes can be found a short distance down this road on the right-hand side.

RIVER WYRE

The River Wyre is much smaller than the two main Lancashire rivers, the Lune and the Ribble. Despite its size it has good stocks of chub, bream, roach, dace and perch. The chub go to over 5lb and there are roach to 2lb and some huge bream and perch.

The Ribble and Wyre Association (made up of the Preston Centre, Wigan and District A.A. and Bolton Centre) have a series of stretches which their members can fish at Garstang, Great Eccleston and St Michael's.

The Garstang stretch runs downstream from the Lancaster Canal aqueduct and runs parallel to Kepple Lane. The stretch at St Michael's is downstream of the St Michael's Bridge, which can be found in the centre of St Michael's, and can be accessed via the stile next to the bridge. There are two lengths at Great Eccleston. The first section is between where the river is close to the A586 and back upstream to the Lower Wild Boar Farm. The second is upstream of the Cartford Toll Bridge.

The Warrington Anglers Association have control of two and a half miles of the River Wyre and its tributary the River Brock. At Churchtown, they have stretches one field downstream from the footbridge and two fields upstream of it. The have several other fields downstream to the River Brock, which joins the Wyre at St Michael's, and 600 yards of the left-hand bank on the Brock. Members are asked to park discreetly in the corner of St. Helen's Church car park at Churchtown.

The Prince Albert AS have a stretch of the river at White Hall Farm, St Michael's.

The Preston Centre and Wigan and District A.A. both produce maps of their fishing rights and I strongly recommend that you purchase one of these as they only cost 50p and £1.25 respectively.

Cost: The Wigan and District A.A. club card costs £16 for adults, £5 for OAP and only £2 for juniors.

The Preston Centre card is £10 for adults and £5 for OAP and junior. Day tickets are £1.50 and 75p respectively.

Membership to the Warrington A.A. is £25 for adults with a £20 joining fee in the first year, £10 for ladies and £5 for juniors.

The Prince Albert AS card costs £66 a year.

Tickets: Day tickets for the Preston Centre lengths are available from Ted Carter's, 85-88 Church Street, Preston. Tel: 01772 253476. Open Mon-Sat 9am-5.30pm, closed Thursdays.

The Wigan and Preston cards are available from most Lancashire tackle shops.

Applications to join the Warrington A.A. should be sent to PO Box 71, Warrington. WA1 1LR.

A membership application form can be obtained from www.warrington-anglers.org.uk.

There is a three year waiting list for membership to the Prince Albert AS. If you want to join the list write to the Membership Secretary at 37 Sherwood Road, Macclesfield, Cheshire. SK11 7RR. Please include a stamped addressed envelope so that the Membership Secretary can confirm by return of post that you have been added to the list.

Close season: The river is closed from 15th March to 15th June inclusive.

WYRESIDE FISHERIES

Jenkinsons Farm, Garstang Road, St Michael's On Wyre.

There is one 60-peg lake at this venue which has an average depth of 3-4ft. There are deeper areas up to 9ft deep.

The lake holds carp into upper double figures, bream to 9lb and tench to 6lb plus. Roach, rudd, perch, golden orfe and a good head of crucians are also to be found in the lake.

Cost: A day ticket is £5 with additional rods costing an extra £1 each. Disabled and OAP day tickets are £4 with additional rods costing an extra £1 each. Night fishing is available and the cost is as above.

Tickets: Pay on the bank.

Rules: There are no bait bans on the water. No spinning. No large fish to be kept in keepnets.

Close season: Open all year.

Disabled Access: Good.

Matches: There are occasional matches held on the water.

Car Parking: Yes.

Toilets: Yes.

Other Facilities: Snacks and bait are available.

Nearby Amenities: Briarcroft Fishery, Hudsons Farm and Toad Hall are all near.

Directions: Following the A6 north from Preston turn left onto the A586 a couple of miles after passing through Bilsborrow. The fishery can be found about a mile and a quarter down this road on the left-hand side next to the WCF petrol station.

Contact: For further information telephone 01995 679695.

WYRESIDE LAKES

Near Dolphinholme.

Wyreside Lakes is unrivalled as Lancashire's premier carp fishing venue. The number of 30lb carp found on the complex is probably greater than in all of the other waters in Lancashire put together. It will only be a matter of time before Wyreside produces Lancashire's first 40lb carp. That is, if it has not already happened before you have read this!

The complex has seven lakes that cater for the carp, pike, trout and general coarse angler. In fact, there is probably something for everybody at this venue.

However, if you are after big carp then this is the place to be. Wyreside's jewel in the crown is undoubtedly the 17 acre Wyre Lake. It holds five 30lb-plus carp. They are Paw Print and Hoover at 38lb, C-Scale at 35lb, Big Lyn at 34lb and Gladiator at 30lb plus and I've no doubt that these fish will have got bigger since I visited the complex. To supplement the big thirties Wyre Lake can boast 11 known 25lb plus specimens. The average weight of the fish is around the 22lb mark. What's more, all of this is available on 24 hour tickets from Monday to Friday each week!

The Wyre Lake has depths ranging from 3ft-12ft and it has an island which is fairly central to the lake. Because it holds so many quality fish, it is not a

Pete Hall with Big Lyn, a carp weighing in at over 30lb

place for the novice or occasional angler. The Wyre Lake is more suited to the experienced and patient angler.

The Bantons Lake is also more suited to the serious carp angler. It is also available on the 24 hour ticket from Monday to Friday. It contains two thirties, Two Bleeps at 34lb and Drop Scale at 30lb plus. There are also eight other known 25lb plus fish. Bantons has a small island which is again quite central to the water. It is slightly deeper than the Wyre Lake with depths up to 20ft. The average weight of the fish is 19lb.

The River Lake is only 2.5 acres and is regarded as fairly difficult carp water. Its largest resident is 28lb with plenty of other fish in the 16lb-20lb bracket. It has depths ranging from 4ft-14ft. It can be fished on a 24 hour, full or half day ticket.

Sunnyside 1 is the 6 acre carp and pike lake. Both species run to 30lb with most of the carp between 10lb and 20lb. The largest pike caught weighed 31lb but there is a wide range of weights with most fish being between 7lb and 25lb. Sunnyside 1 has depths up to 10ft. The end of the lake closest the main car park is quite shallow and on warm days many of the carp can be seen cruising about in the upper layers through the weed and rushes. The lake is available on the 24 hour, full or half day ticket.

The Fox's Lake is the general coarse lake. It is stocked with carp to 16lb, tench and bream to 10lb, roach, rudd, perch and chub. It has 40 pegs and depths to 10ft. Adjoining the Fox's Lake is the Children's Coarse Lake. It is stuffed full of fish with carp to 12lb, roach, rudd and a few tench. Any child under the age of 12 can fish the Children's Coarse Lake for free if they are accompanied by a paying adult. Otherwise the Children's Coarse Lake is half the price of the Fox's Lake. Children must be supervised on the Lake at all times.

The trout lake is Sunnyside 2. This is filled each week with 125 trout of 2lb and so game anglers should expect plenty of action if they get their methods correct.

The complex is expertly managed and all captures must be recorded in the catch log in the on site tackle shop. There is a board detailing the week's captures and running totals for the year. This allows you to see just how well the fishery is doing at the time of your visit. The venue is large and the lakes are perhaps bigger than many other waters you have fished and this can be quite daunting when you are deciding where to fish. The bailiffs are very friendly and helpful so, if you are new to the fishery, do not be afraid to ask for help and advice.

Cost: Wyre Lake and Bantons Lake are available from 8am Monday to 8am Friday and are £18 per 24 hours for three rods. Fox's Lake, River Lake and Sunnyside 1 can be fished with either one or two rods and cost £8/£10 for 24 hours, £4.50/£8 for a full day and £4/£5 for a half day. Pike fishing is £16 per

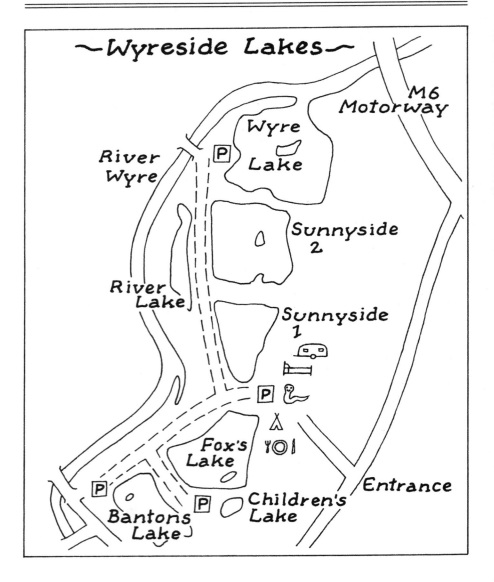

day. Children's Coarse Lake is half the price of the Fox's Lake. Trout fishing on Sunnyside 2 is £16 for a full day with a four fish limit, £10 for a 5 hour period with a two fish limit and £6.50 for 3 hours with a one fish limit. Sporting tickets are £12, £8 and £6 respectively.

Tickets: Must be purchased on entry to the fishery at the tackle shop which you will see to your right as you reach the main car park. The fishery is open from 7am-7pm every day. The last ticket is at 7pm or 1 hour before dusk. Tickets may be booked for up to a week in advance and they are reserved until 10am on the day.

Rules: No trout pellets of any description and no tiger nuts or any other nuts etc. Minimum breaking strain line of 15lb, no shock leaders, running leads only (no fixed or semi-fixed leads), unhooking mats required. Please dip all nets and slings etc before commencing fishing. Barbed hooks only.

Close season: Open all year. Sunnyside 1 is shut during the close season, 15th March-15th June inclusive.

Disabled Access: Good. You can drive your car to most pegs. The management will help make provisions for disabled anglers. Some pegs may be difficult to reach due to the slopes banking to the water's edge. There is a large disabled platform on Sunnyside 1.

Matches: There are occasional matches on the complex but they are rare. The venue hosts the largest Junior Fish-In each year and in 1999 Wyreside was a venue for the British Carp Championships.

Car Parking: Yes. You can drive to your peg, drop off your gear and then park on one of the four car parks on the venue.

Toilets: Yes. There is an anglers' rest room with toilets, sinks and a shower.

Other Facilities: There is an on site tackle shop that sells bits of tackle, boilies and groundbait. (No maggots) The fishery manager has trout rods for hire and tuition can be arranged. The cafe is open at weekends which serves snacks and there is also a licensed bar which is popular with weekend anglers. At weekends there are hot food deliveries to your peg. The service is available between 7pm and 8pm. You can choose from steak sandwiches, burgers, sausages, chips, chip barmcakes, pies, chicken and chips and of course, fish and chips! Drinks, ice creams and snacks may be available from the cafe during the week depending on staffing levels. There is room for caravans which are £5 per night for a pitch and £6.50 if you want an electrical hook up. Tent pitches are £3 per night. There is bed and breakfast at Sunnyside farmhouse and two Scandinavian Pine Lodges that can be booked on a weekly basis.

Nearby Amenities: If you need to leave the fishery then there is the Fleece Inn just down the road. If you prefer more general coarse fishing then there is Woodfold Farm Fisheries, Thursland Hill Farm, Manor House Fisheries, Copthorne and several other fisheries off the A6.

Directions: The fishery is signposted from the A6 and the first signpost can be found 50 yards south of junction 33 of the M6 motorway roundabout. Following the signposts for Wyreside Fishery, turn off the A6 onto Hampsons Lane and follow this road until you reach the crossroads at the Fleece Inn.

Here go straight on and then turn right where instructed by the signposts and the fishery entrance is 400 yards on the left.

Contact: For further details contact Bob and Elaine Birkin at Wyreside Lakes Fishery, Sunnyside Farmhouse, Bay Horse, Near Lancaster, Lancashire. LA2 9DG. Or telephone the complex on 01524 792093.

The author at the Fox's Lake at Wyreside

Also from Sigma Leisure:

ANGLING DAYS

Jack Bevan

Halcyon days are recalled for anglers and all lovers of watery ways in this absorbing personal memoir which will appeal to all lovers of the countryside.

Jack Bevan shares the joys of his angling successes and humorously relives the disappointments, at the same time as he relishes the diverse natural backdrop of his angling excursions: the peaceful Yorkshire Dales, the magnificent Italian Alps, a sleepy brook in Shropshire or a clear stream in picturesque Dorset. Rather than being a 'how-to-do-it' manual, this is more a lesson in how to make the most of your fishing trips. There is an abundant supply of expertise both to help the beginner and satisfy the experienced angler. All of the delights of angling are here, from visiting tackle shops and indulging in flights of fancy about success in the following season to enjoying a river idyll on a wonderful May morning. £6.95

THE CONISTON TIGERS: Seventy Years of Mountain Adventure

A. Harry Griffin

This is the story of A. Harry Griffin MBE, Country Diary writer for *The Guardian*. "A living history of modern Lakeland climbing" – Chris Bonington. "The book which thousands have been willing Harry to write." – Alan Rusbridger, Editor of *The Guardian*. "Prose tumbles off the page as clear as a mountain stream – a classic of mountain literature" – Bill Birkett, mountain writer & photographer. "... one of the great outdoor writers of the century." – Cameron McNeish, Editor of *The Great Outdoors*. £9.95 (paperback edition)

CATHERINE ROTHWELL'S LANCASHIRE COOKBOOK

Catherine Rothwell has amassed a huge collection of recipes - including many old, handwritten ones which have been part of the family life for decades. There are 180 recipes in this book, from simple cookery to sophisticated contemporary dishes - all in a logical easy-to-use format. £6.95

BEST TEA SHOP WALKS IN LANCASHIRE

Clive Price

Walk through breathtaking upland scenery, lush river valleys and along impressive coastal paths and complete your day by indulging in the English pastime of afternoon tea. This refreshing blend of walks and tea shops helps you get the very best out of Lancashire. £6.95

BEST PUB WALKS IN LANCASHIRE

Neil Coates

Join local author Neil Coates in a celebration of the best pubs, beers and walks in wonderful countryside. Tried and tested country inns welcome weary walkers. £6.95

DISCOVERY WALKS IN LANCASHIRE

Brian Conduit

30 routes of varying lengths and terrain, for seasoned walkers and casual strollers. All walks have a heritage theme and enable you to appreciate Lancashire's rich historical legacy as well as its ever-changing landscape. £6.95

WALKS IN MYSTERIOUS LANCASHIRE

Graham Dugdale

Delving into a host of mysterious places throughout Lancashire, this unusual collection of 30 walks, suitable for all the family, appeals to walkers with enquiring minds. £6.95

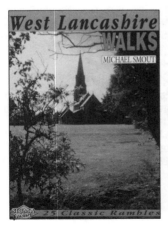

50 CLASSIC WALKS IN LANCASHIRE

Terry Marsh

Terry Marsh reveals Lancashire at its diverse best - from wild woodland expanses and witch country, to tranquil river valleys. £7.95

WEST LANCASHIRE WALKS / EAST LANCASHIRE WALKS *(2 Volumes)*

Michael Smout

No need to venture into touristy areas, it's all on the doorstep for Lancashire's walkers - "Knowledgeable guide to 25 rambles by the Ramblers' West Lancs Group Chairman" RAMBLING TODAY. £6.95 per volume

BY-WAY BIKING IN LANCASHIRE

Henry Tindell

From Morecambe Bay to Bolton and from Blackpool to Burnley, Henry Tindell reveals Lancashire's out-standing potential as a destination for mountain bikers. £7.95

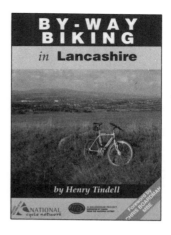

LANCASHIRE MAGIC & MYSTERY:
Secrets of the Red Rose County

Kenneth Fields

Covering all of Lancashire, including Merseyside and Greater Manchester, Ken Field's new book will guide you to places of mystery and curiosity. £6.95

TOWNS & VILLAGES OF BRITAIN:
LANCASHIRE

Michael Smout

The moors, valleys and mossland of Lancashire are the backdrop to this account of the county's towns and villages. Michael Smout is keen to emphasise that Lancashire's austere mill towns often obscure a rich, often eerie past. "The histories of our towns and villages neatly gathered in one definitive guide" SOUTHPORT VISITER. £8.95

CHILLING TRUE TALES OF OLD
LANCASHIRE

Keith Johnson

Set in Victorian Lancashire, here is a spine-chilling collection of tales - "...sure to thrill, chill and amaze" THE LANCASTER GUARDIAN. £6.95

All of our books are available through booksellers. In case of difficulty, or for a free catalogue, please contact: SIGMA LEISURE, 1 SOUTH OAK LANE, WILMSLOW, CHESHIRE SK9 6AR.
Phone: 01625-531035
Fax: 01625-536800.
E-mail: info@sigmapress.co.uk
Web site: http//www.sigmapress.co.uk
MASTERCARD and VISA orders welcome.